M000309731

F*CK ME RUNNING (A BUSINESS)!

F*CK

THE LESSONS I'VE LEARNED FROM TURNING MY MISTAKES INTO SUCCESSES

ME

RUNNING

(A BUSINESS)!

NOLAN GARRETT

LIONCREST
PUBLISHING

COPYRIGHT © 2021 NOLAN GARRETT
All rights reserved.

F*CK ME RUNNING (A BUSINESS)!
The Lessons I've Learned from Turning
My Mistakes into Successes

ISBN   978-1-5445-1881-7 *Paperback*
       978-1-5445-1880-0 *Ebook*

This book is dedicated to every colleague, employee, client, and partner who patiently stood by me while I personally inspected the temperature of far too many hot stoves.

CONTENTS

INTRODUCTION

When I started my business, I thought I knew everything. After all, I was twenty-three and had just finished my degree. What could be so hard? As long as I delivered what the customer wanted, I was sure to be a success. Man, did I have a lot to learn.

What I didn't know could fill a book. So here we are.

There I was, running my company and quickly realizing that I couldn't do it all alone. I had to rely on other people. Yet they didn't seem to understand what I wanted from them.

Why didn't my staff get it? Or more accurately, why couldn't they all be like me, and want what I want?

They didn't have my drive. They didn't have my skills either, or the same drive to develop them. They didn't think like I did or communicate like I did. They didn't eat, sleep, and shower in the business like I did. And they weren't necessarily willing to innovate or take risks. Looking back, they were all acting like... employees.

They weren't accomplishing my goals. Weren't working well together or putting out high-quality work. Some couldn't even manage to show up on time. The problems simmered below the surface day in and day out, and when a client crisis blew up and I expected them to step up, they instead stepped aside and waited for me to come to the rescue. The harder I pushed them the more I found myself saying "Fine, I'll do it myself."

I grappled with how to get everyone on board and take ownership for several years. My first two approaches, which were emotional and intuitive—and straight from the mind of a twenty-five-year-old—were also resounding flops:

1. **I love you guys.** That's right, I hired friends. They wouldn't let me down, right? *They knew me.*

We had beers together—a lot. And if they got a little behind, I'd help them out—show them the ropes, pick up the slack, and teach them how to be just like me. It never occurred to me that we had little in common when thinking about our designs for our lives—*except* beers.

2. **My staff sucks.** Okay, so I (clearly) hired the wrong people, because the business isn't getting what it needs from them. I will just replace them with ready-made staff who *know* what I want, *want* what I want, and can *do* what I want.

I wasn't happy and my staff was even more miserable. I felt like a failure, which didn't make sense because I'd always been an overachiever. But as CEO, I wasn't cutting it. I certainly wasn't working and thinking according to the title.

My first lesson was to stop expecting my team to think like business owners, and to meet them where they were. Further, I had to hold myself accountable—in my role, in my actions, and in my speech—before I could expect any Accountability from my people.

IT'S ALL ON YOU

Being a leader is a challenging job, to say the least. It's not the same as being a "normal employee" or individual contributor, showing up to do a J-O-B, clocking out at five, and collecting a paycheck. The camaraderie you had with colleagues in your previous positions doesn't work when you're running the business or leading a team. You must manage yourself differently so you can manage your people. That's on *you*, not them.

You have to be a leader. They *want* you to be a leader—and more than that, they *need* you to lead them. Not your staff's buddy, not their pal. They are looking to you for guidance, and motivation, and a reason to care. They want safety, too, so they can talk to you openly and without fear of repercussions. They want to know where you're going with the business—where you're taking them. Otherwise, all you're offering them is a job. And if all you have to offer is a job, then all you can expect them to give is the minimum required to not lose that job. What they want—a real leader—is the key to what you need: people you can depend on who exceed your expectations and love doing it.

If you're like many fledgling business owners, you started a company because you have deep skills in your subject area. You're really good at something and decided to turn those talents into a business. If you're a CEO or executive, perhaps you were hired to the position based on those skills. Either way, unless you rose up a chain of command with people reporting to you, you likely have little to no team management experience. That leadership class you took in college doesn't count because when it comes to business, reality and textbooks aren't one and the same. Far from it. Until you are in the CEO's or business owner's position, you have no idea what you're in for.

You're not alone though. In all my years of talking with entrepreneurs and leaders, I can't recall a single person who didn't have to deal with this challenge. People with no business or leadership background start companies every day. Companies promote people like this into leadership roles too. How many times have you seen the top sales guy or gal rewarded by being put in charge of a dozen other salespeople? Sure, they may be an ace at selling, but how are they at teaching other people how to sell? When this new leader fails, the company blames them instead of taking responsibility for not promoting the right person or providing the right training.

You don't have to fall into this trap. You do have to take it upon yourself to prevent it.

Running a business and being a leader goes beyond the relationship you have with your employees. Doing it wrong was one of my first major mistakes, but there were many more: bad partnerships, taking my company's culture for granted, underestimating the power in failure, and getting so caught up in all of it that I forgot to take care of myself.

Finally, I had no idea what an amazing experience being a success could be. I'm not talking about the financial rewards when you're successful, or the prestige, or how cool it is to put the title "CEO" after your name on your business card. There is so much good that is possible for the leader who wants it. Good for your family, for your friends, for your employees, and for your community. First, you need to know what can go wrong so you can get it right.

LEARNING TO REBOOT MYSELF

Like every other kid in the twenty-first century, I planned to be a video game programmer. Majoring in computer science was a no-brainer. A class on information warfare that I took for extra credit made me fall in love with the idea of information security management, so I changed the focus of my degree away from video game development to information security.

Those were innocent times on the old "interwebs." It was 2005 when some computer malware was going around, and people were hacking into websites for fun or recognition. Theft of credit card data was barely on the rise. They weren't stealing health information and submitting false insurance claims. The global cost of cybercrime in 2005 was around $300 million (for comparison, by 2019 the costs were estimated at over $5 trillion). Most businesses got along with a one-person security team—just enough of a presence to keep the company's lawyers happy.

After graduation, I joined a small business that was contracted to perform Information Technology Safety and Soundness exams for every state-chartered credit union in Washington state. Many of these credit unions were small, not particularly technical, and of course, potential attack targets. At the time, information security was not a priority. This was when I became keenly aware of the risks—and the opportunity.

So, in 2007, a partner and I started Intrinium to fill that gap. The idea was to blend security consulting with security management. It turned out to be a smart move because a few years later, the field blew up. I was a cybersecurity guy before security was cool and every IT firm claimed to be a security expert.

We were doing fine for a couple of years with just three employees, but then the business began to grow. My partner left and I brought in more people. Suddenly, I had to figure out how to lead these people and move the business forward. The problem was I knew nothing about hiring or managing people. I had limited experience and my partner had brought in most of the team members based on personal connections. So I did everything you absolutely should *not* do—I hired my friends who had zero experience in what I was asking them to do.

It was a lot of fun for a while—a bunch of friends working together, drinking together, and generally having a good old time talking about how smart we were and how successful we were going to be. Our initial goal was to "Take Over the World." I loved the flexible lifestyle and the camaraderie. I was the accessible, fun boss who picked up the drinking tabs on the company card. But I soon got in over my head. I couldn't count on everyone doing what I did, I didn't want to micromanage them, and I sure as hell did not have time to do the work *for* them.

The business was in endless turmoil. Customers were sending me angry emails: "Your service is not what it used to be. We love you, Nolan, but your staff can't do the work." I lost clients and didn't understand why. Despite all the problems, the industry was exploding, and we were still growing. But with the struggles, for every step we took forward we got knocked two steps back. I couldn't get traction and was barely paying the bills.

I got so desperate at one point that I wanted to throw in the towel. When a competitor made me a ridiculously low offer for my business, for a moment, I actually considered it. Over the next ten years, I entertained other offers, but selected to acquire other businesses (and bring on a new partner along the way) to boost Intrinium's scale, and did a lot of work for large enterprises in California to build up both my business references and my personal resume. That brilliant strategy led to complete burnout.

I took a sabbatical to recover and regroup. Crawling back from career rock bottom, I searched for ways to salvage my business without sacrificing myself. Around this same time, I started getting offers for lucrative CIO and CISO positions, while also being repeatedly approached by private equity (PE) to sell the business. Man, it was tempting. In one fell swoop, I could dump all my problems on someone else and settle into a sweet job, a big paycheck, and a lot less stress. I couldn't do it though. I couldn't walk out on what I had built. I couldn't walk out on my people either. By then, I had around fifty employees. Maybe I wasn't the best leader, but subjecting them to the unknown was worse, and I couldn't shake the feeling that most of the offers I was receiving were from investors that would hollow out the business, lay off the staff, and take the contracts elsewhere. I said no to those offers and made them my wake-up call: fix the business or get out.

But if I was going to make a go of it, something had to change. That something was me. Heading into my mid-thirties, I was drinking too hard most nights, especially when traveling, and sometimes coming home at two in the morning. I wasn't eating right or exercising, generally blaming my "endless travel" as my excuse. I'd show up for work tired, sometimes hungover, and usually feeling like crap. Ready to lead the day. Ha! Before I could ask anyone else to change, I had to work on myself.

I also needed to fix my company, and I set out to do just that. I read everything I could get my hands on, talked to other people who had been there, and hired people to do what I couldn't. I made it my mission to reboot myself and my business to create a healthy, sustainable life, a company I was proud of, and a workplace where people could earn recognition for the quality of work I knew we were capable of doing.

All that, plus turn out kickass services that thrilled our customers. By the time I was thirty-five, I had finally gained enough knowledge, experience, and self-awareness to run a business.

DIRTY LITTLE SECRETS

I wrote this book so you can learn from all my mistakes and avoid making them yourself. On these pages, you'll learn how to communicate with your people, define your company's culture, and eliminate bringing in people who have the potential to destroy everything you built.

At the same time, you'll develop a plan to take care of yourself, which will help you make good decisions. You'll also learn to develop and empower your staff to share and own those decisions—and become leaders themselves.

You'll get the benefit of real-life examples of terrible decisions I made, the consequences, and how I recovered. These are common mistakes—it's just that no one ever talks about them. It's not sexy to brag about this stuff. But if all I put in this book was the good stuff, I wouldn't be doing you any favors.

Instead, I'll tell you the dirty little secrets leaders carry around with them. Because we all make these mistakes. They're common enough that you're bound to run into most of them as a business owner or CEO, especially if you are starting from scratch, as I was. I'm putting it all out there, along with actionable steps to keep you from making the same mistakes.

WHAT'S IN IT FOR YOU

Through real-world stories of my experiences, this book will teach you how to avoid the most common problems entrepreneurs, leaders, and business owners deal with. If you're already dealing with these issues, I'll show you what to do now and how to recover.

Nothing you're going through is unique to you. In entrepreneurial groups, I continually see the same situations across business categories. Every single day, start-up owners are making the same mistakes. Of course, they're embarrassed to admit it, even though there's no shame in being human. But just as soon as someone fesses up, you can count on every other CEO in the room groaning, *Oh, God, I did that too.*

This is the leadership training they didn't teach you in MBA school. You won't even know you need it until the proverbial shit hits the fan and you're stuck with the whole mess. It's not a strategy framework and a bunch of worksheets and metrics and sixteen-letter words that you'll have to look up in your business dictionary. There is no glossary. There aren't any big words in this book at all, and if you find one, you can call me out on it. This is you and me talking, leader to leader, business owner to business owner, CEO to CEO. The BS meter is on.

These are the hard-earned lessons that no one talks about, but you need to know. Unless you're really into pain, but that's another subject, another book.

We're going to talk about your job. Because being a leader is a lot more than you probably bargained for, but you can do it. You *should* do it. Your team *needs* you to do it. Do it well.

I'm going to talk to you about taking care of yourself before you tell everybody else what to do. We'll get into partnerships (oh boy, are we going to get into partnerships) and friendships at work, and company culture. We'll talk about failures too.

If all this sounds too awful and you're already rethinking your career, hang on because we're going to talk about success too. Running a business is one of the most rewarding, honorable things you can do. You have the power and resources to do a lot of good out there in that big, bad world. Stuff you could never do stuck behind someone else's desk in someone else's company.

First, we'll talk about your role: CEO, Leader, Business Owner, Founder, Entrepreneur. Whatever title you have in your signature block, I have a lot to tell you and you're going to be glad you listened.

CEO

IT'S NOT JUST A TITLE, IT'S ACTUALLY A JOB

We all know someone who started a company, got new business cards with the title *CEO* under their name, bought a BMW, and made their first million the next day. Because that's what CEOs do, or at least what some entrepreneurs *think* they do.

I don't know *any* CEOs who started out like that. I certainly didn't.

When I launched my business, I didn't even call myself a CEO. At twenty-three, I wasn't quite sure what the title meant. Instead, I called myself the

Founder of the business. That sounded less pretentious and I actually knew what *that* title meant.

I didn't buy a new car either. My wife at the time supported us and we ate a lot of ramen noodles. Every dollar I made went back into the business, mostly straight to payroll. That went on for two years, but I was determined to turn a profit, and the key was making sure everything was done right. Right as in "under my direction and to my exact specifications."

From my perspective, as the company's founder, I was in charge of everything. My idea of leadership entailed having a complete and full understanding of every activity at all times. I had to know every person's skills, responsibilities, and the details of their performance—even the ones who had managers doing that. It was also my job (or so I thought) to solve every problem, so I inserted myself into every crisis. I thought I was supposed to personally interact with every potential client, so I did sales calls too. I was the go-to guy for *everything*.

Surprise, surprise, that approach didn't lead to the resounding success I expected. It actually had the opposite effect. By engaging in every activity, interaction, and crisis, I was limiting the company's ability to scale. My people weren't too thrilled with me either, as they never had an opportunity to develop. The helicopter-CEO would always be there, ready to solve the most difficult problems.

The role of a real leader, no matter what title you hold, isn't to be the know-it-all and do-it-all. It's to surround yourself with people you can trust, ask them for input, and delegate the day-to-day work and many of the decisions. You also have to give people a safe place to fail if they try and don't succeed. And you have to hold them accountable if they don't give it their best shot. The leader's role isn't one of control, but enablement: giving people the resources they need to do a job well and *getting the hell out of the way*. They might need a budget, people, time, and space, and if you can give them that—and a clear vision of the expected outcome—you have done your job.

As a leader, your measurement of success is not what you do or the recognition you receive for your accomplishments. The ultimate benchmark for success can be measured in the people who report to you—your employees. When they're achieving the business's goals and finding balance between work and their personal lives, you're winning. If you do that, you're not just a CEO, you're a true leader.

Before we get into more details of what a leader actually is, let's talk about some of the myths.

LET'S START WITH THE MONEY

First off, if you think being a CEO—whether by starting a business or being hired or promoted into the role—guarantees you an instant million-dollar salary, forget it. As an entrepreneur, you're still seeing money from the perspective of your personal finances. To you, $5,000 is a good chunk of cash. In a business, thousands of dollars can disappear in the blink of an eye. That's one week's salary for a few employees. It's rent for the month.

Until you've run a business, you have no concept of all the expenses involved. Entrepreneurs go into business thinking that if they get a certain number of customers, they will automatically be rich. They believe the key to financial success is repeat subscribers. That's before they see how many people, organizations, and government agencies have their hands in the company's pocket.

My entrepreneurial ramen noodle experience is typical: you're investing for so long in the business that, if you can even draw a salary, it's probably tiny. Even if your business has a seven-figure total top-line revenue, that doesn't mean you're making much. In fact, you're probably not earning anywhere close to what you could earn in a "normal job" until that revenue hits $5 or $6 million.

If you don't own the company but were promoted into the role, your personal finance picture is brighter because you've got a good paycheck. But you're not getting it just to show up. The pressure's on to earn every penny—mainly by increasing revenue.

THEN THERE'S ALL THAT RESPONSIBILITY

Revenue-earning isn't the only pressure you face as a leader. You're now the ultimate decision-maker. Everyone looks to you for answers and expects you to know how to solve every problem. That's a lot riding on your shoulders that wasn't there before.

People who come to you for answers will give you 70 percent of the context, present two choices, say the deadline's tomorrow, and ask you to pick one. To do this, you'll need to be willing to take some risk because you can't be sure of the outcome. The staff starts to use you as a crutch to keep from taking any responsibility: *the boss said yes, so if it blows up, it's not my problem.* If you don't change that behavior, they'll take up all your time and never learn to make their own decisions or be accountable for anything. So when things go wrong, you might be pointing a finger at someone, but you'll have three other fingers pointing back at you.

IT'S ALL YOU—AND NO ONE ELSE

Finally, it can be lonely at the top, and I've found that condition is generally self-selected. You might start out surrounded by people, but over time, it's easy to end up with virtually no personal life. You won't even notice it happening. I'm no role model in this case. The other day, I did the exercise where you write your own obituary. Then I listed who I thought would come to my funeral—nearly every one of them was a colleague or an employee! Work is where you spend all your time, and if you don't take steps to create relationships outside of your role, you'll slowly but surely feel isolated. Working too much is a big weakness of mine that I've been working on for the past couple of years, but it's still a struggle. If you're similarly afflicted and you ignore it, that feeling could bring you to the point where you don't enjoy being a leader anymore.

YOU CAN DO THIS

The problems may seem overwhelming, but you can do this. Knowing what to expect is half the battle—it's the piece I was missing. I had to learn many of my original expectations were wrong.

First off, if you're starting a business, don't kid yourself about the money side of it. Plan to be broke for a while—maybe a long while. Whether you're an entrepreneur or a leader hired into the role, consider every check you write as an investment meant to get a return. And by the way, don't expect your staff to make that connection—at least until you train them to get it. When I was an employee, all I cared about was getting paid more: *Revenue? What's that?* I asked for three raises in two years. It never occurred to me that to get paid more, I needed to deliver more. When you're in charge of the company's finances, that connection is painfully clear. Knowing this ahead of time will help you avoid any surprises.

Then, grow a decisive team. Set a tone from the start to get your staff used to solving their own problems. Ask questions like, "What are we trying to achieve?" and "What do you suggest?" When they respond, ask them to explain why they suggested it and how it delivers the outcome "we" want. Then you might have to follow up, "Do we need to validate that decision?" "Is there an expert or a client we should talk to?" Get them thinking. Get them to feel accountable.

At first, you may find it hard to resist the urge to jump in and solve every problem. You'll need to practice. It's so worthwhile, though, because encouraging the people who report to you to seek their own approaches to challenges—to take ownership—will pay off every day. Every decision they make will not only give you time to focus on your work, but will also give them a better look at how their day-to-day tasks contribute to the big picture.

The staff, particularly younger or less experienced ones, are likely to find this new skill hard because they fear making the wrong choice. Work through that fear with them—not by making the decision for them, but by creating a safe place for them to make it. Encourage them to experiment. You'll need to constantly balance between holding them accountable to doing their job and letting them know it's okay to fail if they learn from their mistakes. Help them to understand the lesson and ask, without judgment, how they plan to avoid those mistakes in the future. More about dealing with and learning from failure can be found in Chapter 6.

This approach works with skills, too. Let's say I want a sales representative to be able to close large deals, and I feel like he's just about ready to do that. Of course, I would hate to lose any of those deals. To develop his skills, though, I have to be willing to take that risk. I have to provide him with training and resources and create a safe place for him to fail, with mentorship, while he learns. Then I have to get out of the way. If he doesn't learn to close deals after a reasonable period, *I've* learned something. I probably have the wrong person in that role. There's that balance again, and it's hard. But until you do it, you'll be making all the decisions, doing all the jobs, and closing all the deals.

This doesn't mean abdication of all of the effort required to start, run, and grow a business. There *are* going to be important decisions that only you can make—more than you could ever have anticipated when you were an employee. People depend on your judgment. They've staked their livelihoods on it, and with each decision, you're asking them to follow you to a place neither of you has been.

The 2020 COVID-19 pandemic is a perfect example. No one knew what was coming, so every leader was limited to gazing at tea leaves and into crystal balls. But every decision that comes up in a crisis affects your future finances, and there was so much to decide. Trust me, I asked myself a lot of questions and made a lot of decisions during that period:

- Can I afford my staff and avoid layoffs?
- Can we make this investment in our infrastructure?
- Can I launch this product, or should I put some funds into an existing one?
- Should I stop offering this service?

One of the biggest challenges for my firm was the fact that my people *are* my product. We're a service company. My payroll is huge, so when I didn't have enough work for everyone, laying off some people would give me a little profit instead of just breaking even. That was one choice, but I knew that anyone I laid off might not come back. I didn't want to take that risk, so I did everything I could to keep my staff. I bet on recovery.

It's not like there's a one-size-fits-all solution for making all the right decisions (*In Case of Global Unexpected Crisis, Break Glass and Follow These Easy Instructions*) and in this case, there weren't even any data points for support. All you can do is rely on your gut, informed by what's going on in the world, your industry, and your business. It means that more than ever before, you can't look your staff in the eye and promise your decisions will guarantee success. You can give them only the reasonable likelihood that a certain direction is the right one, tell them why, and invite them to challenge you if they disagree. Your staff and your business need you to make those hard decisions confidently and follow through on them.

As you grow into the role, don't leave your friends

and family behind. Maintain those important relationships, or the work will consume you. If you get to the point where you feel lonely or isolated, do something about it. The people who report to you should not constitute your social network. Develop new relationships with people outside of work. That can be hard to make time for when you're focused on building your business. You'll need to make a conscious effort to take breaks from work so you can keep it from becoming your total identity—and avoid the long-term brain damage being "always on" will cause.

THE BIG PAYOFF

Yes, it's hard to run a company and be a leader. It's not what you were used to when you felt like a superstar at your technical/management/individual contributor job. Becoming a leader takes so much more than just getting a promotion or filing a business license. That's step zero on a hundred-step plan. The hard work is about to begin.

Despite the struggles, though, a leadership role can be an incredibly rewarding journey. You repeatedly set goals for yourself and have to rise to the occasion. You may even become financially successful. From my perspective, it's not the money in the bank that matters, it's having the ability to take care of my family no matter what happens, and take care of my staff, making sure they have good pay and benefits and can take care of *their* families. It's also the lifestyle that success as an entrepreneur or executive can bring you: all the good things in life. There are experiences, there's travel, a nice home, a great car, and contributing to charitable work to make a real difference in your community and the world.

Not everyone is capable of being a leader or even wants to be one. You might not care about accumulating wealth. You might not care about making a good life for yourself and your family, or helping other people have better lives. By this point, you may be rethinking your whole career (and considering selling your business or turning in your resignation). But if you can look down the road and honestly say you want to be a leader, that decision will change who you are in ways you could never imagine. In my case, I wouldn't have had it any other way.

QUESTIONS, ACTIONS, AND RESOURCES

Chapter 1 explored my high-level take on being a CEO. Whether you've been in a leadership role for many years or you're new to the job, consider the following questions, actions, and resources that I recommend for a better CEO experience.

QUESTIONS

1. Why are you starting this journey? Are you ready and excited to lead people?
2. Are you ready for the responsibility that will be bestowed upon you as you lead others on this journey?
3. How will you ensure you have balance?

ACTIONS

1. Create a five- and ten-year vision that describes your business and where you fit in it. What will your role be? Will you find that role challenging and rewarding?
2. Make a list: What areas of your life will require stability or improvement before you can lead others?
3. Envision your lifestyle once you've achieved

your goals. Who will you help? How will those you led along the way talk about your role in their lives?

RESOURCES

- Peter F. Drucker, *The Effective Executive: The Definitive Guide to Getting the Right Things Done* (New York: Collins, 2006).
- Seth Godin, *Tribes: We Need You to Lead Us* (New York: Portfolio, 2008).
- Chip Heath and Dan Heath, *Switch: How to Change Things When Change Is Hard* (New York: Crown, 2010).

MANAGE YOURSELF

BEFORE YOU CAN MANAGE OTHERS, YOU HAVE TO GET YOURSELF UNDER CONTROL

For years, I labored—*literally*—under the misconception that I had to do everything myself. No matter how many staff members I had, I was convinced that not one of them could do anything to my standards. Of course, my standards were high, probably ridiculously high.

By 2017, the business had scaled from $100,000 of revenue in our first year to over $5 million a year, and I'd acquired a new partner via an acquisition in 2014. We were scaling like crazy, but my mentality was still in "start-up" mode. I had handed off a few tasks (the ones I didn't like—accounting, anyone?) but was still wearing too many hats. I couldn't let go of the habits I'd formed when it was just my first partner and me, working side by side. I couldn't let go of the work that gave me the most satisfaction, though—the hands-on work that had made me a superstar. I was managing a lot of accounts, involved in projects and technical work, and doing the leadership stuff too, like making decisions and putting out fires. I was working all the time but keeping it together. What could go wrong?

Everything. The entire thing could go wrong. We landed a $2 million per year deal for a single large-scale transformation project. Business exploded. What a seasoned CEO would see as a blessing nearly took us down—took *me* down. We got absolutely slammed, and I responded the only way I knew how: working harder and working more. On top of running my Washington site, I took on the full-time role of CISO for a customer in San Francisco. Nine months later, I took on another role as a full-time CISO for a client in Los Angeles—keeping the role in San Francisco. Flying between cities and states, I was regularly putting in one hundred hours a week.

To make matters worse, a commercial brewery I'd invested in as a side business in 2014 was beginning to fail and required more and more of my time to run the business operations and keep it online while working on selling it. Further, the partner I'd acquired wasn't stepping up to catch the extra work that needed to be done as we were growing, and in fact seemed to be actively sabotaging our success, causing me to have to firefight internal personnel issues on a weekly basis in addition to the external delivery and sales responsibilities I had. I needed help badly, but I was the only one qualified to do the work because I'd never mentored my team, nor made them accountable. That thought had never occurred to me. In my mind, they should just know this stuff, and what they didn't know, they should have learned by simply being in my presence.

I had to talk to them, had to get them up to speed, remind them of what their job was in this company. I had to give them more responsibility. But I didn't. I delayed and delayed and delayed. I stayed in my comfort zone, taking on more work, responding to every emergency. And something happened that had never happened to me before: I started falling behind on my work. And I actually started to resent it. Every text from an employee, a customer—even a simple status update—irritated me.

I was failing. *And* I was burning out. Finally, I started to get it. I began thinking *maybe this isn't what being a CEO is all about*. I had to learn to lead people, not do their jobs, but before I could even get to that point, I had to fix myself. My health was on the downslide, and at the rate I was going, a spectacular crash and burn were just over the horizon.

BREAKING POINT

My breaking point came during—of all things—a fifteen-mile hike with my girlfriend and her family. Exercise was a rarity for me at the time, and I should have been enjoying the break from work. Instead, I spent every mile in my head, agonizing over how I'd ruined my life, wearing myself out for no reward. All I could think about was the letter of resignation I would write to get out of the mess I'd made. Quitting seemed like the only solution.

While everyone else was laughing, talking, and picking huckleberries, I was so pissed off about everything that I couldn't enjoy the hike, these people I cared about, and the beautiful views right in front of me. What was I even doing with my career if I couldn't appreciate days like this? Beyond the few pictures I took with my iPhone, I don't recall much about that hike. It's a blur of misery, anger, and hopelessness.

Back at the house, I went into our room and just fell apart. I cried for an hour. I asked myself the big questions, "What the fuck am I doing?" "What's the point of all this?" I don't tend to be emotional, so seeing me like that scared my girlfriend. I told her, "I don't have much of a reason to live right now." I wasn't actively ideating ways to end my life, but I was completely distraught and felt as though I'd wasted the first ten years of my adulthood on nothing.

The work I once loved and the business I'd built around it had destroyed me. My company was in trouble because it relied directly on me to generate the financial health we were experiencing, and I didn't know how to extract myself without damaging the business, my staff, and my business partner. Even if I had known, I didn't have the energy or the desire. I was exhausted—and ashamed. How was I going to tell people that I had thrown away ten years of my life because I got tired? I'd committed almost my entire career to building a business, yet my state of mind was, *Screw it. The money's not worth it.* I was ready to hand my shares over to my partner and walk away.

I'm grateful that my girlfriend helped me find a therapist. The official diagnosis turned out to be "burnout-related depression"—no surprise there. The therapist helped me see how stupid I'd been and what I needed to do about it. I took a couple of months off—a break from the business to work on *me.* To manage the business, I had to learn how to manage myself first.

YOU'RE NOT A TEENAGER ANYMORE

Once I stepped back, I could clearly see what had led to my breaking point. Aside from all the work, I was living an incredibly unhealthy lifestyle. I ate whatever I wanted to get through the day—they call it stress eating for a reason. I wasn't sleeping well either and I certainly wasn't working out. Any spare time was spent flying home to see friends or flying to Spokane to see my girlfriend.

Whenever I traveled, whether to LA or Manhattan, I brought my gym bag and weightlifting belt, and I stayed at specific hotels that had full gyms. Of course, I never actually set foot in those gyms. Like most traveling CEOs, I stayed out too late and woke up too groggy to even stretch, let alone work out.

Remember those days when you could abuse your body and get away with it? You could live on junk food, stay up all night, and not miss a beat in your day. I hope you enjoyed it (I know I did). By the time you hit thirty, your body will start letting you know, *that's enough of that. It's time to grow up and take care of me.* That's when you have to become intentional about your health—and stay intentional, no matter what—or suffer the consequences.

When life's normal, it's easy to eat well, exercise, and get to bed on time. The company's running smoothly and you can maintain a routine. Throw business travel into the mix, though, and there goes the routine. It's hard to hold on to healthier habits away from home. You tell yourself, "I'll eat well and hit the gym as soon as I get back." But you get home and you're wiped out and you have to be on another plane in two days. So you'll do it the next time, after that trip. Then, the *next* time. Well, next time never comes.

You have to make yourself break that cycle of putting off your health until you're at home, or until you have time, or until work isn't so nuts. When you're in those high-demand situations, traveling and working practically around the clock, you need to be at your best more than ever.

Around the same time, I came to another realization. Whenever one of my staff had complained to me about how they were feeling under pressure, I hadn't taken them seriously. I just didn't get it. Why would they be putting work ahead of their own health?

Yet, that's exactly what I was doing. I was putting my mental and physical health on the line day after day to focus on work. At the same time, I expected to somehow derive all my happiness from work—the very thing that was killing me. Sick, right? Yet, I'm fairly sure I wasn't the only CEO on the planet out there doing this. I'm willing to bet there are plenty still out there doing the same damn thing.

WORKING IT OUT

The real solution—the one that had eluded me for years—was learning how to be happy first, then bring that person to the job. I became intentional about it, trying to answer some basic questions:

What makes a person happy?

What can I do to be more well-rounded?

I read a lot of books on the subject and identified a common thread. Exercise was a big one, specifically cardiovascular training. Cardio increases your brain's gray matter so you can make better decisions. Conversely, overwork, stress, and no sleep destroy those same cells. Clearly, I wasn't giving my brain the fuel it needed. I had to start there because if I couldn't even think effectively, I'd never get myself out of the situation I was in. Cardio training has many more benefits too—the obvious ones around heart and lung health, muscles, bones, and joints. There was literally no reason not to do it.

In what outsiders may call an "about-face," I took a hard line on how I prioritized my health. Health—everything from eating to sleeping and working out—became my elevated, #1 priority. I started eating better, focusing on whole, clean, and when possible, organic foods. Instead of working sleep around my activities, I enforced my schedule for sleep and scheduled everything else around that, focusing on sleeping seven hours every night. I said no to anything that would get in the way of that sleep, like a red-eye flight. And I started training, first weightlifting, then later, adding cardio. Within four weeks, I was becoming a different person. The haze of an unhealthy life had finally lifted, and I could see what I needed to do and how to do it.

First, I had to take control of my haphazard lifestyle. It's ironic how leaders can run entire companies, yet they can't take time to get their own lives in order. The cobbler's children truly have no shoes. The same skills I'd applied to get my business off the ground, I applied to myself, with the goal of becoming a healthy, happy, and more well-rounded, complete person.

In order to set myself up for a good day, I developed a routine that started the night before. Your routine may look different than mine but it's important to have one and stick to it with consistency.

GO TO BED EARLY

If you're feeling the burnout of leadership, your first order of business is to get sufficient sleep. Shoot for at least seven hours. If you're used to just a few hours of sleep and you start getting seven or more, you're going to feel like a whole new person. I'm usually asleep by 8:30 p.m.—no kidding. Going to bed early keeps you from wasting the late hours of the evening and makes it possible to get enough sleep *and* get up early the next day.

WAKE UP EARLY

You need to begin with a consistent, healthy plan for the first hours of the day. Even when the rest of the day gets away from you, your morning shouldn't. An unplanned, chaotic morning puts you in the wrong mindset right from the start. So my "new me" plan began as soon as I woke up. I was never a morning person, but I trained myself to be one. Now I'm up between 4:30 and 5 a.m., without an alarm.

Giving yourself time in the morning before your employees and clients are active and the typical demands start piling up allows you to start the day calm and in control. Otherwise, you're rushing around, spending the whole day trying to catch up, and never feeling really focused.

MEDITATE

Take twenty minutes to meditate in the morning— thirty if you can get the time. I make myself a cup of coffee first, then I start my *Binaural Beats: Meditation* playlist on Spotify, close my eyes, focus on my breathing, and let my thoughts go. There are other ways to meditate and you can do it however you want. Some people use music or an app, or they sit in a certain place a certain way. The important thing is that for the first moments of the day, you are relaxed and allowing your brain to warm up for the day.

WRITE

Every single morning, I write down three things:

1. What I'm grateful for that day.
2. The name of a person—a family member, a friend, an employee, or a client—who needs some support. I take a moment to send them

positive thoughts, and sometimes I think about what I can do or say later that day to show them I care.

3. My primary intention for the day. As an example, let's take today, the day I set aside in my week to write this part of the book. My calendar shows more than three hours' worth of back-to-back, one-on-one meetings with staff members. I also have to squeeze in a call with a potential partner and do assorted other items on my checklist. Yet I still managed to focus on this book. With all that is going on, the book feels most at risk. So, the intention I write is "to be present and focused when I sit down to write." To come up with your daily intention, ask yourself, "If I were to accomplish only one thing today, what's the most critical?" This question helps you rank the possible ways of spending your time in a way that elevates an item you do *for yourself* versus an obligation.

Every executive I know who isn't burned out does a version of this writing exercise and schedules time to decompress. Some of them set aside an hour every day for "me time." They segregate work time from non-work time more than I do. I prefer a more fluid approach because what's most import-ant can be in any category, or categories can even overlap. Fluidity helps you zoom in on whatever has the most long-term impact. It keeps all those ten-minute, instant-gratification tasks that are right in front of you from eating the energy you need for the harder, major stuff.

Writing your intention makes it easier to remember and helps you hold yourself accountable. When I open my notebook to write, I see yesterday's writ-ing and think about whether I accomplished my intention. Before I close it, I spend a little time thinking through the likely challenges that might prevent me from meeting my intention that day.

KEEP LEARNING

The next half hour to an hour of the morning is spent reading about leadership, my industry, or what's going on in the world that I need to be aware of as CEO. Audiobooks or podcasts are other great mechanisms—the key is to ensure you've put some new ideas and information into your brain for the day.

WORKING OUT

Never underestimate the value and necessity of regular exercise. Physically fit people are more resistant to colds, flu, and diseases. You can't afford to get sick, but if you do, being in shape allows you to bounce back more quickly. Regular exercise is also an investment in your life as you get older. I'm not a doctor, so take it from the studies: high-intensity cardio training changes your brain to keep it younger and more resilient to deal with the demands and pressures facing any leader. High-intensity cardio also keeps you alert and less likely to tire out. When you're physically or mentally worn out, you can't effectively lead, and no amount of Mountain Dew can make up for being out of shape. In fact, guzzling sweet, caffeinated soda just leads to a sugar crash—then you're even worse off than when you started. Put in some time on a treadmill, stair stepper, bike, or trail in the morning, and you'll find yourself losing your desire for those carbonated beverages that do nothing for you but counteract the work you're putting in to be healthy.

You don't have to do your workouts in the morning, but be sure to do them. I decided to start running. That might not sound like a big deal, but I used to be the guy who said the only time you'd catch me running was if a bear were chasing me. To me, running was the worst activity in the world. At first, I forced myself, but I soon learned that with enough motivation, repetition, and time, you can change your perception of anything. You can basically rewire your brain. I planted the thought, *I like running,* and I ran. Then I would tell myself, "That was fun." One day, about four weeks into running at least three times weekly, a crazy thing happened: I woke up *wanting* to run.

If you don't want to run, do something else that gets your heart rate up. If you want to think clearly, make sound decisions, and actually look forward to work again—instead of dreading it—choose a cardio workout and make it a habit. Add strength training to your routine too. I alternate running (or some alternate moderate to high-intensity cardio) and lifting weights six days a week and take one rest day.

At first, you'll feel a little awkward telling yourself and your staff, "Yes, I see the business is on fire. Again. I'm going for a run." The idea of taking time to invest in your physical and mental health seems counterintuitive when your go-to knee-jerk reaction is to double down. It may feel like procrastinating. Keep reminding yourself that what you're really doing is becoming a better leader.

Enhanced physical health isn't the only reward when you exercise. You may find yourself opening up to more activities. Maybe you've never thought of yourself as a hiker, a camper, a sailor, or a martial artist. Suddenly, you could be. Physical activity gets you out of your head and can lead to social relationships that help you defeat the feelings of isolation that affect so many leaders.

Even though I grew to enjoy running, I still don't like it as much as *not* running, and I don't like lifting weights as much as *not* lifting weights. If I thought my health could stand it, I'd skip them. But there's power in doing something you don't want to do in the morning. It sets a mental tone that you can do anything. Once you start to actually like running, or lifting weights, or whatever you choose, you might feel compelled to take on something else that you don't like to do. If you start your day with that one thing—a five-mile run, thirty bench presses—the rest of the day looks a lot easier. You'll be thinking,

I handled that; I can handle anything. What else ya got? Bring it on!

You'll find it easy to come up with a reason not to work out, so be prepared to counter it. Find a way to hold yourself accountable. Remind yourself how valuable you are, not just to the company, but to yourself, your family, and your friends. Remember this, too: you were born into this world to be a complete human being. Religious considerations aside, the only thing we can know for sure is that you get one life—and one body—on this earth. Consider it your responsibility to make it the absolute best it can be.

GET TO WORK

Finally, I take a shower and get to work. A lot of people would fit breakfast in there, but for the first few years I was an intermittent faster on the weekdays, and frequently skipped it. I typically ate just one meal a day, in the early evening. The main point of the morning routine is so when you get to work, you really *can* get to work. You're energized, focused, and ready to take on whatever smacks you in the face.

Pro tip: while the intermittent fasting diet worked well initially, as I expanded my weightlifting regimen and stepped up my cardio, I found that intermittent fasting was no longer a fit for the number of calories I needed to consume, and I found my irritability was pretty high in the afternoons before I got to my meal. In 2021, I've switched to scheduled three-day fasts once per quarter and regular three to five meals per day to achieve the caloric intake I need for my current weightlifting routine. The point is, do what fits your exercise regimen and provides the best results for your body.

SELF-AWARENESS AND CONTROL FOR EVERYONE'S SAKE

Being in control of your life with a morning routine and exercise builds self-awareness, which puts you in a better position to see situations from other people's perspectives. Otherwise, you're just drinking your own Kool-Aid, and that doesn't benefit anyone. When you start to believe your own BS and expect everyone else to go along, you're not being a leader. It's like the CEO who's always "selling" their company to every client or new recruit. They start to believe their vision is the only reality that exists. You have to keep reminding yourself it isn't. That self-control and awareness help you get out of your head and understand how other people view issues, challenges, and conflicts.

For a long time, I didn't get that. I believed the goal I had set for the company should matter to everyone, and I was frustrated when it didn't. I couldn't figure out why people weren't working as hard as I was to reach it. Why *wouldn't* they want to help me build an Inc. 5000 (or even an Inc. 500) company? It was just Nolan alone on his journey and I didn't understand why. I had lost perspective.

I had to learn to realize that my employees' and clients' priorities were not the same as mine. Then I had to understand what they were. I trained myself to do this by resisting the urge to simply react, and to instead step back and ask myself, "If I were an outsider asked to mediate, how would this problem look to me? What are the perspectives, realities, and goals of the people involved?"

Determine the answers to these questions and you can begin to bridge the gap between where you're trying to go and how to motivate other people to help you get there.

SET BOUNDARIES

Sticking to routines requires setting boundaries to protect your time. Otherwise, you'll get distracted by that important email or phone call (which, in hindsight, could have waited till you got into the office). Boundaries protect your psychological health too. That means taking time for yourself to disconnect. Parkinson's Law states that work expands to fill the time allotted. At work, this translates to, *If you leave your calendar open to everyone, they will fill it with their priorities, which may not be yours.*

It took me a long time to learn that lesson. I thought the key to efficiency was to make myself available to my clients and staff whenever they needed me. I took calls and instant messages on evenings, weekends, and in the middle of the night. I was actually proud of a ridiculous habit I had created for myself: *review and/or respond to every email in thirty seconds or less.* I stuck to that rule all the way up to 2017, when it became impossible to manage.

I had to learn to separate life and work and make myself available when it made sense to be available. For me, that was seven hours a day, five days a week.

I let people know my schedule, and if they accidentally book a meeting outside those times, I ask them to reschedule. I even defined which "emergencies" qualified as acceptable for invading my boundaries, and you would not believe how much more my staff was able to do without me around to make all the decisions and take all the actions. They turned out to be intelligent problem-solvers, and the business didn't implode. Imagine that: vetting, hiring, and training the best people you can find, only to discover they're just as capable as you thought they were the first day you met.

PROTECT YOUR THINKING TIME

At one time, a lot of companies adopted an open-door policy. Executives would allow anyone to pop into their office at any time for any reason. A closed door meant you didn't appreciate and respect your staff enough to allow them into your inner sanctum. While that's a lovely theory, in practice, it sucks.

A CEO needs time to think. And they need alone time to do that without feeling guilty about it. You can't be creative, strategize, or solve a complex problem with people popping in and out of your office. I enjoy talking to my staff, but I need time to do work that requires solitude too. So I close my door when I need to, and I don't feel bad about it. My staff understands.

I recommend closing your door as often and as long as it takes to really focus on what you're doing and make sufficient progress on it. Multitasking isn't really effective—your brain doesn't work that way. Remember when you'd try to run too many programs on a computer that didn't have a lot of memory? We used to call that "thrashing" because programs were just getting switched in and out of memory, but none of them were in memory long enough to actually do anything. That's what it's like when you try to do more than one thing at a time—your brain is thrashing from one task to the next, and never processing anything.

All of that refocusing of your brain wastes a whole lot of time, consumes your executive function, and wears you out. Meanwhile, you accomplish nothing. Okay, maybe not nothing. But your productivity is diminished, and what you do manage to accomplish doesn't reflect the degree of quality that you could bring to it if you were able to give it your complete attention. On top of that, multitasking, cognitive switching—whatever you want to call it—takes an emotional toll. Those interruptions make you feel anxious, and that makes it even harder to think.

Limit your availability, close your door when you need to, and if you have a bad phone habit, break it. There is no law requiring you to have your phone on—or even on you—twenty-four hours a day. Put it away when you're with other people. Stash it in a closet or drawer at night. Your phone shouldn't be the last thing you see at the end of the day or the first thing you see when you wake up. If you're worried about emergencies, set it to only ring when someone calls you three times.

This all sounds easy, but it's not. Being busy, on-call, and ready to solve every problem at a moment's notice can turn into an addiction. You get a rush, a high, from being so productive. After all, getting things done is what leaders do best, and it feels great to have those little successes throughout the day. If you're addicted to work, society is happy to enable that addiction. There's so much emphasis placed on hard work and success that it's practically a moral pillar. Work is such a big part of the American culture, and nobody tells you it's not good to work all the time. Leaders often get their identities so tied up in their jobs to the point of feeling guilty when they relax.

I used to hear this a lot: "Wow, you're so hard-working. It's great that you started a company. When do you even sleep? I'm so impressed!" Those comments only reinforced my behavior. If you don't watch out, buying into those compliments locks you into a reputation you feel pressured to maintain.

There's nothing unhealthy about feeling personal satisfaction from your successes. But they're not always the right kind of successes. Answering an email or text is not a monumental achievement. It's usually nothing more than a reaction. Even closing a deal that your salespeople could close is nothing to brag about. You're smarter than that.

GET BACK TO YOUR WHY

Establishing and defending boundaries and reg-ularly disconnecting from habitual "busy-ness" will drive your creativity and put you on the path to happiness. Although it may sound counterintuitive, working less is likely to result in a net efficiency gain in the long run. Not a single successful leader I know has ever said, "What's important to me is being able to work as many hours a day as I can." What you should care about is adding value for every hour you spend.

Remember why you chose to be in your role in the first place. If I were to ask you why you're doing this, I doubt you'd say you love being anxious all the time because you have too much to do. No, it's probably more like, "I'm doing this because I want to be successful," or "I want to make money to buy the home, car, and lifestyle I want," or "I want to have discretionary income or time to give away when I feel like it," or "I want a flexible work life and more time for travel, family, and friends."

Every now and then (now would be good, or right after you finish this chapter) take an hour to revisit your ultimate "whys" and goals. Write them down. Whatever they are, make sure you're protecting your ability to deliver those returns.

I do a goal-setting exercise once a year, asking

"What do I want to achieve next year?" I write separate relational, intellectual, financial, and health goals. I do this because of what I've learned along the way: the work you're in the middle of will make you feel as though it'll always matter, but it won't feel the same to you in twenty years. Your priorities should evolve with time. I've found that Darren Hardy's *Living Your Best Year Ever* planner is a great place to start, especially if this is your first time creating an annual plan for yourself.

CURB YOUR WORKLOAD

Setting, communicating, and protecting strong boundaries are only part of the leadership challenge. Once you have that "work time" partitioned off, you must figure out how to make the best use of it. As I've mentioned, it's too easy to take on tasks that aren't yours. Be honest and reasonable about how much you can do, should do, or even want to do.

I'm not saying you should be a jerk and start saying no to every request. I am saying that despite what you believe, you probably aren't the only person in the company who can do that audit (guilty), head up that new technical implementation (guilty), or close the deal with that new customer (guilty). Yes, I was guilty of all of those. Doing those things made me feel like a hero. I was actually just competing with my staff and depriving them of the opportunity to get some experience and have a turn at wearing the cape.

Once you have the means to hire more people, learn to delegate tasks, ownership, and Accountability. Be like a consultant in your company. Staff should come to you for advisement, to brainstorm, and to work on problems together. Don't take the Accountability for achieving the goal away from your staff. As the leader, it's not your job to directly ensure the company hits its sales numbers: That's the sales manager's job. It's your job to ensure the sales manager is successful and achieves the outcome of hitting the sales targets by providing tools, time, mentoring, praise, criticism, and any other resources required for their success.

If that sales manager tries to palm off the ownership and Accountability on you, remember your job and your boundaries, and say, "No, this is on you. You are accountable for the outcomes. Your job is to tell me their status. Let me know if we're not going to achieve them, and we'll talk about what to do and how I can enable you to win."

Be there to provide tools and the benefit of your experience to your managers and staff. Do they need more people? Money? Time? Ideas? Once you all agree on a plan, the onus is on them to execute it and take responsibility for the outcome. That includes letting you know (before things go south) that something is going off course.

Be the leader your people need and deserve. Put your staff on the path to their own wins, instead of keeping the biggest ones for yourself. Give credit where it's due, and make sure the person who gets it isn't you. Take your satisfaction in your title, your income, and your staff's accomplishments.

If you ever feel like succumbing to the temptation of hoarding the wins, remember this: that ego boost you feel comes at the expense of training your staff to do their own jobs so you can spend your time building the company. Eventually, it will cost you your best staff.

DON'T FEEL BAD ABOUT IT, CHANGE IT

This behavior is often driven by ego, or by an addiction to the work and the wins, but not always. In a start-up, leaders often have to wear a lot of hats to get the company off the ground and making enough money to hire the staff they need. That was my story for the first three years. We were only four people, bootstrapping without investment, so I couldn't *not* be working on generating revenue while cranking out production for the clients we already had. I had no choice but to straddle the roles.

If I've described your world, sure, keep straddling—until it becomes feasible to hire and train people to take on the work. Just be ready when the time comes to intentionally let go of that job. You're not there to show off your talent and feel awesome. You're there to be a leader and help others grow their talent beyond yours.

You also need to, as they say, *get a life*. I'm still working on rebuilding the social life I gave up when I was blindly dedicated to my business. I still don't do enough that's unrelated to work. When people ask me what I do, I still start by talking about my work identity. I look forward to getting to a place where I first share my social identity.

HOLD EVERYTHING!

How are you feeling right now? You should be excited by the prospect of handing off some responsibilities and developing the skills you need to lead your staff and run your business. You could be feeling a lot different, like maybe this whole leadership thing isn't for you. If you're dreading this shift, you could be in the wrong role. Being a CEO (or any kind of CXO) isn't for everyone. As cool as it is to have that title on your LinkedIn profile, if the thought of giving up your old job to step into this new role doesn't appeal to you, it's time to do some hard thinking. How do you want to spend your time? Were you happier doing the technical work?

There are always tradeoffs in life. If you're miserable as a CEO, maybe you just need to get better at it. Then again, you might prefer to return to your previous role. There's no shame in that. Staying in a leadership role that you hate isn't fair to your staff or your company. You won't be able to lead them or scale the business. And you'll be miserable. No matter how many hero moments you have, no matter how much money you make, you'll never make the mental leap to becoming an effective leader while maintaining a staff mentality.

By the way, if you own the business but don't want to run it, you can hire a CEO and still maintain that business owner status. You can even stay involved with the day-to-day work. You just can't lead the company. Give this some thought, decide what you want, and lean into it.

YOU'RE MORE THAN A LEADER

Let's say you're *there*—managing yourself so you can be the leader people need. You have a daily routine that gets you in the right state of mind, keeps you healthy and fit, and sets you up for a productive day. You've developed self-awareness and control and created boundaries. You've even decided exactly how much you want to give to your leader role—and it's not 100 percent. That doesn't mean you aren't giving 100 percent when you're leading, but that there is more to you than being a leader. As a human, an individual, you have more to experience and contribute to the world than running a business.

So, what are you going to do with the rest of you?

What you do is up to you. If you're new to leadership, hang onto the friendships and interests outside of your professional role. Business has a way of consuming people, especially people who are really good at it. You have to intentionally commit time to other people and activities. If you've already been sucked into the "all business, all the time" mindset like I was, figure out what makes you happy. What have you done in the past that gave you the same "high" as a big win? Or what have you always wanted to do?

When I was younger, I played in rock bands. There was nothing like meeting up in a friend's garage and jamming with my best buddies. Building new songs gave me a chance to engage my creative side too. So why did I give that up? I don't even remember when I quit music. It wasn't an active decision, it just kind of faded away—and I missed it. So, after fifteen years, I picked up my guitar. Actually, I went digging around in the basement for it, dusted it off, tuned it, and was relieved to find that I still remembered some chords. Then I called around. Was anyone up for getting together every couple of weeks for a jam session at my place?

Whatever it is you're doing now, keep doing it. Whatever you've lost, you can get it back. You can also find more interests. It took me years to discover that I didn't have to be just Nolan the CEO. I could be Nolan the guitar player, Nolan the runner, Nolan the author.

This is not about reclaiming your youth. It's about being a whole, well-rounded person so you can be a whole, well-rounded leader. Existing in a leadership vacuum sacrifices all those unique qualities that differentiate you from all the other leaders out there. Explore those. See what you can learn from them. Bring those lessons to your position. It will add a new dimension to your role and separate you from the pack.

Just joining an entrepreneurs' group doesn't cut it. Networking is all good and fine, and I heartily support engaging with other leaders and business owners. It feels good to talk to people interested in the same things you're into, and you can learn a lot. You can also get sucked into a sort of groupthink, reading the same books and blogs, listening to the same podcasts, and paying allegiance to the same thought leaders. If that's all you're doing, you are not *flexing*—you're just doubling down on work. There is more to you than that, and you need to find it. Expand your horizons.

If you don't do this, life will get away from you. The years will fly by, and while you're having another discussion with another CEO about business, finance, information security, and industry trends, something will happen. You will become boring.

Sure, your entrepreneur group buddies will want to talk to you. Your employees, who you pay to listen to you, will pay attention when you speak. But no one will really want to engage with you on any other level, because you will have lost the ability to have a conversation about anything beyond work.

If you're into sports, that's a starting point. Most people like to talk about their favorite team. Personally, when people start talking about "last night's game," my eyes glaze over. I've never been a spectator, but that doesn't mean I can't find a sport I like and become an active participant. I still remember how to throw a ball.

The personal benefits of stretching yourself are obvious. Those other activities are like a release valve, where you just kind of let all the air out of your leadership role and relax. You don't always have to be in charge, and it's better if you're not in charge of those other activities. Let someone else take on that role. And because you aren't 100 percent focused on business, people outside of work might actually want to hang out with you.

When they do, you can interact with them in a way

that's creative and rewarding. At the office, your role is to be the leader, not a friend. But outside the office, you're more free to show your friendly and funny side. You can enjoy the feeling of not being in charge, which is essential to becoming a balanced person.

Ironically, letting your whole self play outside of work makes you a better leader and connector at work. In particular, I find I'm better at interviewing and recruiting since I've made time for a social life. The old me came off as someone who was just all about work. I failed to recruit some good people because of my inability to engage. It was not for lack of trying. I just had nothing to say on a human level because work was my life. No banter, no sports knowledge, nothing.

Although I don't watch sports—I'd rather swing the bat myself than see someone else do it—I've added snowboarding and skiing to my repertoire. It's all a result of my decision to become a more well-rounded person. In addition to snowy slopes (and reading), I also find a fresh perspective in my social groups, and you should, too. Get together with people outside your industry as much as you can.

I'm also in an entrepreneurial mastermind group, but it's with a bunch of dentists. I get a lot out of how differently they think than people in my industry do. Random insights come from what they talk about and how they approach challenges. Dentists improvise. If a tool they need doesn't exist, they'll go out and make it (as in literally, with a 3D printer). That doesn't tend to happen in technology leadership.

DO IT, OR SUFFER THE CONSEQUENCES

If you don't get serious about investing in your well-being, you'll have only one voice in your head: the one constantly telling you to do more work. Add a morning routine, an exercise routine, and other dimensions to your life and you'll be able to quiet that voice.

It took me a long time to get here. I got so burned out I was ready to give up a multimillion-dollar business and thirteen years of my life just to make the anxiety go away. You can save yourself—and your staff—from all that stress, that suffering, that burnout. Don't blow it.

As you take better care of yourself, you'll be in a

better position to build and sustain good relationships. This is true for your personal life, but it's just as important for your professional relationships.

Next up, we'll get into the most important professional relationship in your life: the one you have with your business partner.

QUESTIONS, ACTIONS, AND RESOURCES

Chapter 2 comprised some of my best advice for getting your act together to manage yourself before you start trying to lead other people. I learned most of it the hard way, but you don't have to. Ask yourself these questions, take these actions, and then read more on the subject. I've listed a few of my favorite books on self-management.

QUESTIONS

1. What are you doing instead of what you *should* be doing?
2. What one part of your routine can you improve immediately?
3. What are your signs of burnout, and what is your

action plan to prevent it when you start to feel the symptoms?

ACTIONS

1. Map out your "perfect day" on a piece of paper or on your schedule. What would have to change to turn your perfect day of self-care and mindfulness into your "every day?"
2. Practice replacing the question "How will *I* get this done?" with "*Who* will get this done?" in your daily vocabulary.
3. Find an accountability partner—and hold each other Accountable.

RESOURCES

- Ray Dalio, *Principles: Life and Work* (New York: Simon & Schuster, 2017).
- Darren Hardy, *Living Your Best Year Ever* (Oregon: Rearden, 2019).
- Aubrey Marcus, *Own the Day, Own Your Life: Optimized Practices for Waking, Working, Learning, Eating, Training, Playing, Sleeping, and Sex* (New York: HarperCollins, 2018).
- Cal Newport, *Deep Work: Rules for Focused Suc-*

cess in a Distracted World (New York: Hatchette, 2016).

PARTNERSHIPS

In August 2015, I was at DEF CON, the biggest hackers' conference out there. I'd gone every year for ten years. It's *the* hacker event of the year.

Summer is always my company's weakest quarter, but it had never looked as horrible as it did that year—a year after I'd acquired a competing business and a 50/50 partner to go along with it. I remember sitting in the hotel in Las Vegas thinking, *I can't afford to be here. Where the hell did I go wrong?*

I knew the answer, but I just didn't want to admit it. My company was in trouble because of a stupid decision I had made.

I'd underestimated the impact that the wrong partner can have on a business.

If you're thinking about taking on a business partner, do not skip this chapter. Understanding the impact a partner can have on your company will save you a lot of money and headaches.

It could ultimately save your business.

SO YOUNG, SO HOPEFUL, SO NAÏVE

My first partner left the company just a couple of years after we launched. For a long time after that, I was the sole owner. Eventually, our local competitors started consolidating and increasing their market share, and I worried that if we didn't scale, we'd get squeezed out of the market. I got all fired up about seeking an acquisition. One of my goals for the move was to bring in skills we lacked. By diversifying our competencies, we could provide a broader stack of services and play in more markets. I also wanted to get my hands on a data center. That would allow us to do some hosting, build more products, and create another recurring revenue source.

I started looking at a company that was a competitor we consistently outperformed. In terms of revenue and staff, they were half the size of Intrinium. But their data center—Linux, Unix, and hosting— seemed to make up for their deficiencies. We were Microsoft partners, focused on remediation and security in that area. I figured they could give me the expanded technical competence I needed to scale. Motivated to make it work, I took the owner out to lunch to talk with him about my goals. Stewart was older and had been working in the region longer, yet he didn't seem to be as well-known or as respected as I was. Those facts—the company's underperformance and the owner's lack of name recognition in the market—should have been a big red flag. But Stewart told me his business was healthy and revenue was consistent. The business was running so smoothly, he said, that he didn't even need to be involved in the day-to-day operations.

That, by the way (in case you're counting), was big red flag number two. How is the owner of a fifteen-person company not involved in the day-to-day? Somehow, I either didn't see the signs (Danger! Danger!) or I chose to ignore them. Instead, my thirty-year-old brain was thinking, *Maybe this guy knows something I don't. After all, he's older. He must be smarter.* Not once did the thought occur to me that I had been running my business just fine without a partner for seven years.

Stewart seemed like a guy who could help me figure out how to grow, so I pushed for the deal. Instead of listening to the signals I was getting, I kept reminding myself that I wanted to grow to fifty people, a hundred people. Hell, I wanted to be the next Deloitte! I repeated this vision over and over to myself and to this new partner who was going to help make it happen. Funny, I never noticed the silence that followed. He never once said those magic words, "That's what I want, too."

Much too late, I realized this person I had partnered with to achieve my long-term growth goals actually wanted the opposite. Stewart didn't want to grow. He didn't even want to work. He wanted to roll his entity into mine, trade out his shares, collect some of mine, and extract that new value when he sold out. Stewart was looking for a way out of his business, and I was going to be his exit ramp.

On paper, his numbers looked good. But without

his daily management and future investment, his business had the minimal potential to sustain itself. In fact, without immediate intervention, it would struggle—something he failed to mention. The signs were there. I just wasn't looking for them. I was seeing only what I wanted to see: additional scale for Intrinium.

Intrinium's revenue had doubled every year since its inception, nearly all of which was organic growth (we'd had one very small acquisition to acquire a remote office on the other side of our state). Six months before I acquired the new company, I stood on my deck and bragged to a friend, "Everything we do turns to gold." My limited experience (and maybe a little bit of ego) told me I was some kind of genius. I had always succeeded and would continue to succeed. Any issues that came up with the acquisition, I could fix, right? That's what I told myself, anyway. My ego got in the way of my common sense.

I rode that "you're so awesome" wave, believing my own bullshit—until it knocked me on my ass. Because that's what happens when you go into an acquisition and 50/50 partnership without true, deep, due diligence.

I signed the paperwork and we merged companies on the first day of 2015. I couldn't wait to take advantage of the new efficiencies and find ways to get our two groups working together.

I immediately rolled the new, managed IT services people into our group. Yet I noticed something odd: the staff was paid based on hours they billed, but there was no verification system for tracking those hours. They just plugged their time into a spreadsheet and assigned the costs to customers at the end of each month.

As you can imagine, that process left a lot of room for creative accounting. I looked at the body of work being done, and the number of hours billed, and it didn't add up. I found instances of people billing four hours for a password reset! That's just one example of many. The staff was working a few hours a week and billing a full forty hours, justifying it however they could. The thinking was, "What will drive the outcome I want (maximum pay)?" and never "What's fair to the customer?" As long as there was no Accountability and the customer didn't complain, there was no incentive to do otherwise. Moral compasses notwithstanding, of course.

This did not reflect how we operated at Intrinium. I had never treated our customers this way, and the thought of a customer finding they'd been over-charged horrified me. As soon as the problem came to my attention, I worked with my director over the department to put the staff on a ticketing system that automatically tracked their time.

Now I had a cultural problem on my hands. The new staff didn't like working more hours for less money. They took the attitude that we—the acquiring company—were a bunch of jerks. So now these people with skills I was looking to leverage, all wanted to leave. In hindsight, the fact that they were cheating customers should have clued me into their char-acters and made me question their technical skills, but I didn't consider that at the time. I was worried about staffing and wanted to keep them on. I should have shown them the door.

THE COLLAPSE OF REVENUE

Now that we were charging customers fairly, within sixty days, revenues from that side of the business were cut almost in half. About a third of billing from the new business was still valid, mainly from cloud services and the data center, but that was it, and this portion of the business didn't have year-over-year growth. The loss couldn't have come at a worse time. Even though the economy in the rest of the United States was pumping along, Spokane suffered a weird, regional economic depression. We were getting squeezed, and the acquisition's revenue imploded. Suddenly our costs were upside down. We were spending more than we took in. By the middle of the first year with my new partner, we both had to pull money out of our personal savings to make payroll. By the end of the year, almost every dollar I had been counting on, based on the profit and loss statement that Stewart had shown me, had evaporated.

Only then did I start to figure out that Stewart and I had vastly different perspectives on business growth and strategy. He had no interest in investing in resources and taking on some risk to grow revenue. Instead of figuring out how to increase sales, he nitpicked every dollar spent.

We'd get a big lead that might bring in up to $200,000 a year, and Stewart would shut it down over items like meal expenses and airfare for our sales rep to close the deal. Investments with an ROI more than ninety days out were shut down. Locking our wallets cost the company a lot of potentially lucrative opportunities and access to high-quality, skilled resources.

The discovery of the time-charging issue should have been red flag number three because it pointed to either a lack of Integrity or a lack of oversight. But up until that point, I thought he was innocent. The whole thing had been going on without his knowledge, right? I thought I knew Stewart, and I believed I could trust him. I had never been wrong before. That's the kind of hubris that takes down a business faster than you can say, "Wrong partner, wrong company, wrong move."

Of course, Stewart wasn't really to blame. He saw a good thing and went for it. This was on me. I was the acquiring partner. I should have done my homework, and I never should have done the fucking deal.

SHOULD I STAY OR SHOULD I GO?

Sitting in my hotel room at DEF CON with time

to think, I realized that my hasty acquisition was endangering the financial health of the business. After many years of success, I was back to square one: managing expenses like I had a start-up.

The writing was on the wall. Without drastic steps, we were headed straight for disaster. As I saw it, there were two options: One, I could sell the business while the previous year's P&L looked good and just go to work for another company. Or two, I could keep the business, dump my partner, and work my butt off to put things right.

Instead, I chose a hybrid of the two: I kept the business and my partner, *and* I got a job. Well, I got two jobs, actually.

One of our clients, a large healthcare system in the Bay Area, needed a full-time CISO. I figured the job would put me in line for an SVP position while letting me pump some much-needed cash into my business. I moved to San Francisco and took the gig under an Intrinium contract. About six months later, I started working for a second California healthcare company in Los Angeles, also as a full-time CISO. For approximately eighteen months, I was traveling between states, doing a crappy job of running my business in Spokane and unaware that my partner was basically torpedoing the company I'd built.

The thirty-five people I'd started with before the acquisition were still doing an amazing job. Some had been with me from the start, originally hired for $30,000 a year. Now they were getting screwed over because I was barely around. I felt as if I'd abandoned the people who had helped build the company, and yet the work I was both doing and bringing in for others was all that was sustaining us.

Some of my best people were threatening to quit if I didn't return and protect them and the company from the partner I'd left in charge. Staff called me in tears, crying about how much everything had changed. Juggling two full-time jobs, running a business (sort of), and dealing with my staff was too much. I clearly remember telling one of my people, "You're going to have to learn to work with him."

I'm not proud of who I was back then. With so much pressure bearing down on me, I made some bad decisions. That's not an excuse, and I take full responsibility for everything that happened. Thank goodness I came around and did something about it before it was too late.

CHILL OUT AND ABOUT FACE

I had to deal with my partner. I had to take care of my business and my people too. But by then I was so burned out that I had to work on myself before I could do anything else. First, I concentrated on making the two healthcare organizations self-sufficient so I could extract myself over time. Then I took a three-month sabbatical to decompress, refocus, and craft a strategy, which was cut short by a month as in my absence, my partner found new ways to create bigger fires.

Dealing with my partner was going to be tough. We were 50/50 partners, so we had to agree on everything. I couldn't fire the guy or force him to sell me his shares. The only way to fix my business was to get him out of it. I needed to reclaim a culture of Integrity and Accountability in the company and get my staff and myself in line with that culture. Stewart was never going to fit into that culture, and having him around just undermined it.

I talked with him the way I should have so many

years before. Over the course of six months, we had multiple, intense conversations. "Stewart," I said, "I want to spend the next ten to fifteen years of my life building the company into at least 500 people and $500 million a year in revenue." Okay, that part was no different from our first chat, but then I added, "Do you want to make that journey with me?"

He said, "Yes. I can get behind that."

FROM NAÏVE TO GULLIBLE

Holy shit, I thought, *I did it! This is amazing. I should have just talked to him like this years ago. We're finally on the same page.* All my problems would soon be solved. *Halle-freakin-lujah!* I wanted to celebrate.

Unfortunately, it was short-lived. A month and a half later, Stewart showed me a plan he'd put together to sell the business. He had shared P&Ls and other business information with various merger and acquisition and private equity companies and had come to an agreement with one of them. And he'd done it behind my back. He pushed some papers toward me and said, "You just have to sign this."

Oh. My. God. I was speechless. Flabbergasted. Mortified. What in the hell was going on? I was buried in work, trying to save our customers and our revenue, hang onto my staff, and turn the company around. I had actually believed him when he told me he was on board. Now this bombshell.

I shut him down immediately. That didn't dissuade him though, and over the next few months, he kept bringing me new deals to consider. These weren't even good deals either—really, in hindsight, this guy wasn't just extractive, he also couldn't see the big picture.

Despite my misgivings and repeatedly communicated lack of interest in a sale, eventually, he worked up a decent deal with a private equity company. He convinced me to meet the potential buyer in person. It was immediately obvious that this individual was nowhere near qualified to make the transition, and I began to fear for the livelihoods of my staff. I was not going to sell, and several weeks later I let the interested party know. Stewart was furious—I had ruined his plan. This was the best offer we would probably get, and I straight up killed it. On the spot, he offered me his shares for a 20 percent discount off the PE offer. To this day, I think he thought I would turn him down. Instead, I stood up, shook his hand, and said, "Thank you. Please transition all of your responsibilities and data to me, and I think it would be best if the staff primarily saw me as the owner going forward."

That day, I began reducing Stewart's access and started the long process for procuring a $5 million loan—the most the SBA allows. That's what it cost me to get Stewart out of there, and it was worth every damned penny.

It took six months to get the financing worked out on the loan to buy him out. At the end of it, he asked me to throw him a going-away party—at my expense. You can't make this stuff up. We did have a party—he just wasn't invited.

YOUR BUSINESS IS YOUR BABY

A partnership is like a marriage, and the business is your baby. You need to be on the same page about how you'll care for it and what you want for its future. You might both agree on the making money part, but how you make it and what you do with it could be miles apart. How much they want to be involved can differ from your vision too. They may be looking to scale up the business but scale back on their contributions to it. Or, like Stewart, they may be looking to leverage the success of others and extract a portion of that value.

Before you say, "I do" to a partner, make sure your goals align. If you're the only one committed to the long haul, your partner could undermine you. If you want to split, it may not be easy. Unlike a marriage, you can't just file for divorce. Both parties have to agree to call it quits.

The big mistake was getting into a partnership with a guy I didn't really know. I ignored all the warning signs, didn't ask the right questions, and when I did ask questions, I heard what I wanted to hear. Basically, I failed to do my due diligence.

PARTNERSHIP DOS, DON'TS, AND ESSENTIAL QUESTIONS

Looking back, it's easy to see what I did wrong. At

that moment, it wasn't so obvious. If I had stopped worrying about the competition, stopped wanting to grow at all costs, and instead focused on what I was really trying to do with my business and the best way to get there, I could have avoided my partnership disaster. I should have invested time learning what to do, what not to do, and what questions to ask.

PARTNERSHIP DOS

Research your partner and make sure you fully understand the person, their business, and how they run it.

- Read their financial statements, including their M&A (mergers and acquisitions) history.
- Interview their staff.
- If possible, interview some of their ex-staff, particularly managers or executives.
- Interview some of their clients.
- Verify their references and claims. (I found out much later that my partner never got the degree he put on his resume. That's right: this guy who was playing CFO at our business didn't have the wherewithal to complete his degree—and then lied about it.)

- Take it slow and test the waters. Before you sign into a partnership, find a way to work with your potential partner to check your compatibility. People may act one way in a meeting, but you won't really get to know them until you put in some time together.
- Have the uncomfortable conversations, the really tough ones you want to avoid because you're afraid you might uncover a deal-breaker. Again, think marriage. You wouldn't wait until after you were married to ask your spouse how much money they make, or how much debt they have, whether they want kids, or whether or not they plan to keep working after you're married. Imagine being surprised by the answers to those questions!

PARTNERSHIP DON'TS

Of all my mistakes, the biggest one I will never, ever repeat is going into a 50/50 partnership. Knowing what that means and knowing myself better, I would never agree to own less than 51 percent of a business I'm running. Unless I'm joining as an investor or a board-level advisor, I need to be in charge. Someone has to say, "the buck stops with me" and if I'm in charge, I want that person to be me. When multiple people have that responsibility, you end up at a lot of impasses. Here are the don'ts I wish I knew when I made my partnership mistake:

- Don't let your ego control your senses.
- Don't leave the physical company for an extended period.
- Don't sacrifice your values.
- Don't ignore culture and how merging, acquiring, or being acquired will affect your staff. People always want to know how changes will affect them, and they typically expect the worst.
- Think long and hard about agreeing to go 50/50 with anyone. Base the decision on what you know about yourself. Equal partnerships work out only when one of the partners wants to leave the decisions to someone else. Somebody has to be the ultimate decision-maker.

QUESTIONS YOU MUST ASK A POTENTIAL BUSINESS PARTNER

Before you ask the person the following questions, answer them yourself. Get crystal clear about them. Then find out how close you and your potential partner are to all of them. Don't assume your goals and values align. Talk about them, then talk some more, and get documentation to back up what you hear. Of course, if they decide to lie, you can't hook them up to a lie-detector test, but your due diligence should catch them. Ask them key questions, including these:

- How does your P&L work?
- How does your billing work?
- Tell me about your technical operations.
- Where do you see the business in five years: how much revenue, how many employees, how many markets? (I did ask those questions, and his answers showed he had no fricking clue what he wanted to achieve. Once again, though, I let my ego get in the way: *Great, I can be the visionary, and he'll be the operational guy.*)
- How do you define success? If the person defines it differently than you do, consider that a big, bloody red flag smacking you in the face. Do not ignore that flag. (During our first lunch, my soon-to-be partner bragged that he had run his business for twenty years and was making about $200,000 a year. He seemed to consider himself at the top of the income stack. I'm not

judging that income, but his perception of success didn't match mine at all: I could easily get a CISO job for double that income without the headaches of owning a business. Instead of seeing that as the deal-breaker it was, I glossed over it.)

- What's the contact info for the last three customers you onboarded?
- What's the contact info for the last three customers you lost?
- How would you describe your company's values?
- How would you describe its culture?
- What are your end-of-career goals? Do you plan to retire? If so, when? What do you want in terms of income and lifestyle? (You want to find out, say, if their dream is just to own shares and sit on the board forever but not do the work.)

The absolute number-one questions you must ask:

- Have you had partners? If so, who are they, and how can I reach them? (You'll learn a lot by talking to them or by your potential partner's unwillingness to put you in touch. What I could've learned from my guy's handful of ex-partners!)

WHAT TO DO ABOUT THE WRONG PARTNER

If you're already in a bad partnership, you still have options. What they are depends on your arrangement. The best scenario, of course, is being able to work out an amicable split. It's best not to burn bridges if you can avoid it.

If that's not possible, if you're the majority partner, the other person can't hold you hostage. You can value the shares and forcibly buy out your partner.

A 50/50 partnership that you can't get out of the nice way leaves you with two options: (1) You can severely overpay for your partner's shares to get yourself out of the deal; or (2) you can make the office environment so uncomfortable for them that they'll leave. As horrible as that sounds, it's better than overpaying a partner who's already extracted undeserved value from your business and/or damaged it, like mine did.

By uncomfortable office environment, I don't mean that I pooped on the guy's desk. I didn't even mold his stapler in Jell-O. Nothing like that. I actually reshaped the culture of the business, which I'll tell you about in an upcoming chapter. Once I had established the company's core values and got the staff focused around them, they stopped following orders from this guy who clearly did not represent them. Within a few months, they were ignoring him. He could see that there was no place for him. The few remaining staff he had brought with him got the same message, and they either left or we let them go.

If you own less than 50 percent of the business, you may not want to leave. Hopefully, you went into it knowing that a minority owner doesn't set the standards and the pace. You should not expect to get your way all, most, or even some of the time. If you didn't think that through when you partnered, and you're not happy now, you still have a couple of options: (1) bring in a coach to help you work out the situation with the other owner and see if they're willing to let you have more say in the decisions (more on this in Chapter 4); or (2) offer them an attractive price for your shares. The price should depend on how motivated they are to buy you out.

In every case, just running away shouldn't be an option. If you find yourself playing with that idea, also consider that you could be forfeiting all the time, effort, and money you've put in. It would be like just abandoning a bad marriage. You need to resolve it so you can fully move on.

KNOW YOUR PARTNER

In a business partnership, you spend more time with the other person than you do with your spouse or your best friend. You have to make a lot of hard decisions together. There is money involved—often, a lot of money. Other people's lives are affected by those decisions. Before you agree to take on a business partner, you'd better make damn sure that you have a strong relationship with the other person, and you'd better be 100 percent crystal clear on each other's expectations and desired outcomes for the business and for yourselves. You'd also better write all of that down so there are no misunderstandings, assumptions, or confusion whatsoever. You will be holding each other accountable for this agreement, so get it all out upfront.

If I had done this, I would have been on the same page with my partner or—if we were both being honest—realized from the get-go that Stewart was not the right partner for me. Then, if one of us went off in a different direction, the other one could say, "Hey man, hold up. This is not what you said you wanted for the business. What's going on? We need to talk." The agreement would have served as a touchstone for our expectations going into the partnership, and I wouldn't have been caught off-guard. Just talking about it isn't enough, because people remember conversations differently. You have to get it all out there, and you have to write it down.

ULTIMATE LESSONS

Ending my partnership with Stewart might sound like it was a tough decision, but it wasn't. Once the writing was on the wall, I knew what I wanted to do—what I *had* to do. The lesson learned was difficult, though. And painful. And really expensive. But it was a lesson that paid off for me personally. It took me on a path I may never have explored. I learned how important it is to take care of myself, be true to myself, and know what I'm getting into when I expose my company to business partners.

Business relationships impact you and your company in ways you could never imagine. This is true for partnerships, and it's also critical in the relationships you have with your employees. From recruiting to hiring, onboarding to training, managing to promoting, you have to be just as clear on what they want out of the deal as you are with what you expect from them. You probably know where this is going: I did not get my relationships with employees exactly right the first time around.

QUESTIONS, ACTIONS, AND RESOURCES

In this chapter, you got a glimpse into what can go wrong with partnerships. If you're considering taking on a business partner, I strongly recommend you ask yourself these questions and take these actions. For more guidance, check out my recommended reading on the topic.

QUESTIONS

1. Why do you want to have a partner, or multiple partners, in your business? Be brutally honest.
2. If you have a partner, how will you ensure a high-quality decision for your business when you disagree?
3. What are the core principles that you will not

compromise on, that your partner needs to be aware of? What about theirs?

ACTIONS

1. Build your touchstone document. Why are you in this business, what are your goals, and what are the roles of yourself and your partner(s) in the business? Seek agreement with your partners.

2. Get a coach. Relationships, particularly ones with ego and money involved, aren't in the honeymoon phase forever. A good coach can help ensure your partnership is strong and grows stronger.

3. Set up monthly one-on-one meetings with your partner, specifically offsite, to cover not just the business but how well you are working together. Practice Candor—Respectful but clear honesty.

RESOURCES

- Rand Fishkin, *Lost and Founder: A Painfully Honest Field Guide to the Startup World* (New York: Portfolio/Penguin, 2018).
- Patrick Lencioni, *The Five Dysfunctions of a*

Team: A Leadership Fable (San Francisco: Jossey-Bass, 2002).

- Simon Sinek, *Start with Why: How Great Leaders Inspire Everyone to Take Action* (New York: Portfolio/Penguin, 2009).

YOU'RE NOT IN THE
FRIENDS BUSINESS

I had never managed anyone before I started my business. Now suddenly I had employees, and I had to figure out what to do with them. In my infinite, twenty-three-year-old wisdom, I figured the best way to manage them was to look at what I wanted from a boss when I was an employee.

I didn't consider that I was never a typical employee. My attitude had always been, *Don't manage me. Just tell me where we're going, and I'll get us there before you can even ask how it's going.* During my first years as a business owner, I assumed everyone I hired felt the same way. Hiring friends was convenient, and since they were all self-starters like me (right?) we'd succeed by communal effort.

Are you seeing a pattern here? It's the same magical thinking I applied to choose a partner: assuming other people thought like me, worked like me, and wanted the same things I wanted. It's how I treated every decision. I didn't for a moment consider how very, very different individuals can be (I guess that's why they call them *individuals*)—or how inviting them into the workplace could impact my vision for the business.

I expected my staff to have my same entrepreneurial mindset. Of course, I wasn't prepared to give them any ownership in the company or even a decent wage. We were a start-up. So think about it: why would anyone like me want to work for me? They wouldn't. They'd start their own business and try to get me to work for them. Yet, I was managing these people as if they were all self-managed, self-motivated, and dying to make my business a success. Not that they were bad people or even bad employees. They just weren't the people I assumed them to be. They weren't Nolan clones. Imagine that.

They were, however, my friends. I assumed they knew me better than anyone. They, of all people, would understand what I wanted, what I was building with my business. I wouldn't have to explain it to them, or set any expectations, or engage in any sort of people management at all. Whatever they didn't know, surely they would absorb it through osmosis after work. Over beers. Where we celebrated our awesomeness.

And since we were such good friends, they'd work their butts off for me.

KILLING WITH KINDNESS

That first year, it became clear that the entry-level tech work was bogging us down, making it hard to scale. I brought in a guy I had never met, who turned out to be a hard worker and a great person. We became fast friends.

Mark learned quickly and was dependable, and I wanted him to succeed. So when I needed someone to run my network services group, I gave him the job. I assumed he was prepared for it, and that he wanted it. Because, again, everyone's like Nolan. Not once did I consider whether he had any people management, or project management, or operational management experience. Or if he even wanted to have those experiences. I never asked him what he needed from me to do the job, never thought about *his* vision for *his* career, *his* future. Mark trusted me, so he thought he could—and should—do the job too.

I wanted to give him an opportunity. Instead, I nearly gave him a heart attack. After nine months of struggling with that job, he was at the dentist for a routine exam and was told, "Go to the ER right now. Your heart rate's through the roof." The guy was only twenty-six years old!

Because we were friends, I'd inadvertently given him a job beyond his abilities. Because we were friends and he didn't want to disappoint me, he was reluctant to speak up and say, "Hey, Nolan, I can't do this. I don't even want to do this." Anyone else would have quit within a few weeks, but he stuck with it because we were friends. We hung out together. Our wives hung out. He was one of my best friends, yet my lack of leadership (because when it comes down to it, a true leader doesn't treat people this way) nearly killed him.

My motivations were pure. I really did want the best for Mark; I just didn't understand what his "best" meant. Instead of just promoting him, I should have said, "Here are the requirements of the job. Do you have the skills? Do you want the responsibility?"

By this time, customers were threatening to leave. Mark wasn't taking care of business, and the pressure was mounting. His four-person staff was pissed, too, because their manager didn't know how to manage. Fresh out of college, these people wanted a mentor. Instead, he was doing the work. He didn't know how to communicate his expectations to them. He didn't know how to determine whether they had the skills. Mark didn't even know how to figure out what skills they had and what they wanted to do with them. Does that sound familiar? Yes, I was quite the role model back then.

Worse, I was oblivious to what Mark was going through. Note to self: When you ask an employee why something isn't done yet and they look like they want to crawl under their desk and curl up in a fetal position, that's a red flag. When one of your people is working eighty hours a week—not on a one-off basis, because you're in a time crunch on a major project, but *week after week*—that's a red flag. The signs were there, and I ignored every one of them. Until Mark became physically ill, I didn't realize the seriousness of the situation or take responsibility for it. I had to offer Mark a way out.

I demoted my friend. This put him at the same level as his former staff, and as much as that hurt his pride, it had to be done for his health and the health of the business. I took no pleasure in the task—just thinking about it kept me up at night, made me feel like the worst friend and boss in the world, and made me question all my other leadership decisions. This was my failure, not Mark's. I explained that to him, hoping he'd see that I wasn't just patronizing him, but that it was true. I had fucked up royally, and my mistake had impacted a lot of people. Our friendship, surprisingly, survived the fiasco. I guess that's a testament to how much we cared about each other and the strength of our bond. Had I kept him in that position, I'm not sure that our friendship (or Mark) would have lasted.

THE INSIDIOUS NATURE OF MIXING FRIENDSHIPS AND BUSINESS

Starting a business is scary. You take a leap of faith with your money and sometimes the money you can't afford to spend. I bootstrapped my business with 1,500 bucks on a wing and a prayer. And a lot of stress. Knowing how hard it would be to go it alone, I reached out for help. My first instinct was to engage people who I believed were already aligned with me and what I wanted in life: my friends. I figured they would be the perfect employees— that we'd work side by side, make a lot of money together, and celebrate the business's success over beers.

In the back of my mind, I was also thinking that if I failed, my friends would stick by me and share the emotional burden. After all, they liked me. They cared about me. In tough times, my friends wouldn't abandon me. Regular employees might. I've known countless entrepreneurs who harbored these same thoughts. It's only when you reflect on those hiring decisions that you realize how misdirected they are. By misdirected, I mean stupid.

In the first place, you can have a close relationship

with only so many real friends. When your business is small, sure, you can take everyone out for beers to celebrate. Or commiserate. But once you get to a dozen or so employees, you don't have the bandwidth to engage in a meaningful way on a day-to-day basis with each and every one of them. When you get up to about fifty people, you will be lucky to have time to say "hello" to everybody. Logistically, it's not possible. So which employees get to be your friends, and which ones have to settle for a smile and a wave as you breeze past their cubicle?

This is a minor issue, though, because the real problem with hiring friends is more insidious, and potentially damaging to your friendships and the company. A successful business relies on the Accountability of its people, from the CEO to the executive team, management, individual contributors, and even the part-time receptionist. You cannot afford weak links in the chain of command. Holding an employee accountable to meet a project deadline that could win or lose a client is a whole different deal than meeting them for lunch. As long as a person sees you as their friend, they will not feel accountable to you to the degree required at work. If you try to enforce it, you won't be able to maintain the friendship.

You know your friends on a personal level. You know what they're doing outside of work. You probably know their families. So one Saturday afternoon you're in your marketing manager's backyard with both your families enjoying a barbecue. Your spouses get along great and they're planning play dates for the kids. Everything's peachy. The next night, you and your IT manager and spouses go on a double date. You all hit it off so well, you might even take a vacation together.

Monday morning, you find out that your friend the marketing manager screwed up the campaign rollout. Also, the network went down over the weekend and your friend the IT manager didn't have anyone on call to deal with it. You know that your friend could have worked out the kinks in the campaign over the weekend, but he was in his backyard flipping burgers. Your IT manager could have called someone or taken care of the network herself, but she was sipping Margaritas on the deck at your favorite restaurant.

Guess who gets to have the difficult conversations and pick up the pieces? Those talks are painful enough to begin with, but now you have to tell these people—your employees, who also happen to be your friends—that they're not getting that bonus, they could be demoted, and you might even have to let them go. How is that going to play out in your office?

I've had these conversations, and in the spirit of honesty and candor, I made it clear that whatever happened would not affect the friendships. I'd get it all out on the table: "This is not going to change what we have outside of work, and me and the wife still want to join you and yours for that barbecue (kids' playdate) (shared vacation)." Ah, the best-laid plans and all that. The conversation never goes that way. Because in my head I'm thinking, *You may feel differently after I say what I need to say. You may not want to hang out with me after I demote you. You probably won't be thinking about a vacation after I let you go.*

And that's how it actually plays out because fumbling through those words feels phony and meaningless. Despite what you say or how pure your intentions, people hear you as a boss—when they thought you were their friend. A sense of betrayal hangs over those conversations like a dark cloud. There's discomfort, awkwardness, and tension, and no matter how many times you go out for beers afterward, the feeling persists. It's baggage that never goes away.

You may even start to question your priorities, weighing friendships against business: *Should I give people a pass when they screw up because I know them personally? Should I hold off on the tough talk until after next week's golf date?* Reading this, the answer is obvious: Hell no. But when you're in the middle of it, the answer's not so easy.

These situations aren't just bad for employees and the business, they take a toll on you too. Deciding how to handle them and dealing with the stress around them takes an incredible amount of time and emotional energy that you should be spending on your business. You can avoid it, though. Just don't hire your friends.

PITFALLS OF MIXING FRIENDS AND BUSINESS

Hiring friends is tempting for a lot of reasons. Unless you're seed-funded and have millions in the bank, you're starting off on a tight budget. I started my company with $5,000 in my checking account after taking out $1,500 to cover the basic business startup costs. Recruiting people you don't know is tough when you can't "show them the money," but friends are a lot more trusting. They believe you won't scam them, and of course, you don't want to scam them.

Bringing on a "friendly audience" makes starting a business a little less scary too. Friends won't criticize you. They won't tear you down and deflate your confidence. Friends tell you you're doing a great job, sometimes even when you're not.

None of these are good reasons to hire friends. In fact, they are reasons you should *not* hire them. Want more reasons? I have plenty because I learned the hard way all the ways bringing on the wrong employees can take your business down.

INCOMPETENT STAFF

Friends who come to work for you don't take the job because it's what they want to do with their lives. They may not even know how to do the job, or at least do it well. The job is a paycheck, not a career. There's no incentive for them to improve in the position either because they figure you'll never reprimand, demote, or fire them. Even the best people will do this. It's not intentional; it's just what happens.

NO WAY TO REPRIMAND

Trying to give serious feedback to an employee who also happens to be your friend rarely ends well. Either you hold back because you don't want to ruin the relationship, or you barge ahead and destroy the friendship. And if you really think the person you just reprimanded, who now hates it, is going to work harder for you after that conversation... well, it doesn't work that way. More likely, they'll want to work less, undermine you, or leave the company.

FAVORITISM

When I started the business, I'd take my friends

out for beers after work. As the company grew, I couldn't take everyone out, so my original crew became the "in crowd"—Nolan's after-work buddies. Don't think the other employees didn't notice. They believed my friends got more support at work and could get away with doing less work.

My actions created distrust among the staff too. People were afraid to share openly with their colleagues for fear that anything that got back to my friends would eventually make it back to me. And it did. Not only did I *not* dissuade the behavior, but I welcomed it too. I had snitches in the company who reported every bit of gossip to me. It didn't occur to me once that I was only getting their perspective, or that everything they told me was coming to me secondhand. I didn't consider that these people— my friends—might have their own agendas, either.

I rejected every accusation of favoritism, claiming that people were being petty or jealous. Thinking about it now, I realize how immature my behavior was, and I realize the impact it had on my staff. People need to be able to talk freely, even vent and complain occasionally. They're not freaking robots, they won't always be happy about their jobs, and they won't always like you. Accept that, and don't worry about it. Honestly, do you love your job every single day? Do you love the people you work with every single day? Do you, the business owner, never ever vent?

Playing favorites is childish. Being secretly privy to the "noise" and responding accordingly does not make you a good leader. It doesn't take the place of creating a strong vision and leading people toward it. If anything, it promotes distrust. When your staff stops trusting you, they begin to question your character, your motivations, and your ability to lead.

UNREALISTIC EXPECTATIONS

You know your friends' strengths, but you're probably blind to their weaknesses. They may not have the skills you need or have the same professional goals. In a traditional recruiting scenario, you'd find out by reviewing a candidate's resume, calling their references, and interviewing them. When the person is your friend, you are less likely to properly vet them. They're not likely to clue you in, either, because they don't want you to think less of them, and they really don't want to jeopardize their job prospects. The usual frank conversations you have as friends do not carry over to the workplace.

They may often bring a sense of entitlement to the workplace like they're doing you a favor working for you, so you should not ask too much of them. They could expect perks the rest of the staff doesn't enjoy, like taking long lunches, leaving work early, or getting extra days off. Every time they push you for that extra favor, your opinion of them will be affected, and your company will suffer.

HANDICAPPING STAFF AND THE COMPANY

Breaking the news about pay and staffing changes to any staff member is hard, maybe among the hardest conversations you'll ever have. When friends are involved, it's a whole lot harder.

When I demoted my friend Mark, I felt so bad that I didn't even have the guts to cut his salary. And remember, his staff—now his coworkers—were still being paid below-market wage at my underfunded start-up. I figured the company would just have to eat it, but it wasn't just about profits. Other people doing the same work at the same level were being paid much less, and that wasn't fair to them. This wasn't fair to Mark either. Rewarding him for not speaking up to ask for help, not letting me know he was in over his head, or not figuring out how to get up to speed, was a disservice to him. It gave him more money in the short term but affected his career development with "golden handcuffs" that didn't motivate him to advance his professional skills. My leadership failure in that situation bothers me to this day.

I also hurt the company financially. Today, $30,000 doesn't seem like a lot of money. At that time, with our meager revenue level, that much cash mattered. I could have used it to reinvest in other portions of the business, with improved infrastructure and software—even a new hire. I was trying to scale, but giving in to my emotions slowed the business down.

COMMUNICATION BASED ON RESPECTFUL CANDOR, NOT FRIENDSHIP

Jack Welch, the former CEO of General Electric, had a lot to say about being a good leader. In conversations with your staff, he recommended being honest and direct while remaining open to the other person's perspective. Welch advised approaching people with candor as if you're their coach.

In some ways, I think of "coach" as another word for "candor" because a coach has to communicate openly about their expectations and each player's commitment. A coach's candor also prevents them from being overly empathetic. They understand the person's point of view but don't allow a player's emotional excuses to overwhelm the reason for holding them accountable. A coach is candid about where a player isn't measuring up.

Don't confuse Respectful Candor with having a license to ignore employees' feelings. You're not there to vent, commiserate, or empathize. You are the leader, and ultimately, the problems are yours. Now it's your job to lead the person toward a solution.

When you talk to your staff about failures, keep your emotions intact and don't just dump the problem and all the consequences of it on them. Give them a chance to respond. And leave the word "you" out of the conversation. Otherwise, your words can feel like an attack.

Compare this phrasing: "Jill, your network went down over the weekend, your customers' software updates didn't go out, people are calling and threatening to cancel, and your screw-up may cost us hundreds of thousands of dollars. What are you going to do about it?"

To this alternative phrasing: "Jill, the network was down all weekend. We need to tell the customers what's going on. How quickly can we get those updates out?"

Let the person know, without blame, that you're in it together, and give them a chance to deal with the immediate problem. Later, you can continue the conversation:

"How did this happen and what can we do to prevent it from happening again?"

Establishing a relationship based on Respectful Candor allows your staff to see you differently too. They don't fear you; they respect you. They don't take advantage of you or try to "gaslight" you either because you've made your expectations and their responsibilities clear. There are no misunderstandings. When an employee makes a mistake, they own it: "Yes, I committed to that, and I failed. Here's how I plan to resolve it."

MOTIVATE PEOPLE THE RIGHT WAY

I thought I could motivate people to work hard because they were my friends. That didn't work out—it never works out. Relying on friendships to inject motivation gets really messy really fast. Even if it works, you're limited to motivating only your friends, which limits your ability to scale. Promote healthy, professional relationships by putting a candid communication process in place. This in turn promotes healthy forms of motivation.

One of my executives, Randy, had a very candid— although initially disappointing—conversation with me. He told me that even though he had agreed to run his department for a year, at six months in he was losing interest and wanted to leave the position. His departure would cost the company money and we both knew it.

I could have said, "Fine, Randy. Your happiness is more important than the business" and just let him leave. I could have said, "You're going to cost me a lot of money" and tried to guilt him into staying. I didn't say either of those things. Instead, we discussed the consequences of his decision. The company would suffer a dip in profits. His leaving would affect the bonus compensation plans of our controller and VP of operations, who are incentivized on profitability. Randy had just hired a guy who had a lot of promise and with some mentoring, could in time become a manager—maybe even take over Randy's position someday. That wouldn't happen if he left.

By painting an honest picture of what would happen if he followed through with his decision, I changed Randy's perspective. He didn't just think, "Nolan wants me to stay because he's a selfish, greedy asshole." He understood the situation he was putting me and the company in, and the effect that his leaving would have on his colleagues and his team. He agreed to stay for another six months, but it was *his* decision. I didn't browbeat him—I showed him the facts and let him make up his own mind.

That coaching moment shows the value of Respectful Candor and of sharing decisions, rather than ruling unilaterally. The experience made him a better leader in general, even after the fact. Leaders have to see the impacts of their actions on everyone who looks to them, everyone whose livelihood depends on them. The outcome improved his ability to make more strategic decisions that considered his entire sphere of influence. His growth as a leader freed up more of my time to focus on scaling the business.

MAINTAIN RESPECT, ACCOUNTABILITY, AND DISTANCE

Work itself can be emotional. You have to connect with people and let them know they can talk to you, but you are not their therapist. Create boundaries and maintain them. If a staff member is involved in a fender bender on the way to work that's going to make them late for a meeting with you, they should call and tell you. If their girlfriend just dumped them and they need a shoulder to cry on, they should not call you for that shoulder.

There's a line between connection and attachment. Some people will try to cross that line to gain favor. Typically, these are people who are struggling at work and hoping that creating a personal bond will protect their job. Don't play that game. Whether you're in the office, at a work-related event, or out for beers with your people, maintain your professionalism and don't give people a reason to lose respect for you or an opportunity to take advantage of you. If a staff member tries to cross that line, provide them with resources, but don't engage in therapy. You can't carry their burdens and successfully manage your staff. Human Resources may be able to help identify resources.

I didn't get this at all as a young CEO. In fact, I didn't have an HR person because I didn't think I needed one. I was everyone's friend and therapist. I didn't even set boundaries for people who weren't my friends. In hindsight, when I realized people were trying to turn our relationship from professional to personal, I should have had a Respectfully Candid conversation with them about my responsibilities as the CEO. Namely, that it was my job to run the business, and that was my number one job. Making friends wasn't even on the list.

Eventually, I learned my lesson about boundaries at work, but I still got mixed up in a relationship that demanded one of those very candid conversations. The guy's name was Brad, and I met him through my girlfriend at the time. Brad worked in a different field and for a different company, and we hit it off well. I was pretty proud of myself for finally making a friend outside of work. By then, I'd also stepped away from micromanaging people at work, so I wasn't aware of every detail of everyone's day-to-day schedules. Imagine my surprise when I discovered Brad had been hired into my company.

As soon as I found out, I sat down with him and explained our respective roles at work and how there could be no crossover between our friendship and working relationship. I was the boss and I didn't play favorites. I'd learned my lesson and wasn't going to repeat that mistake. Brad said he understood, and he seemed to—at first. But after a while, he pushed that boundary. He'd try to get me to intervene when his manager made a decision he didn't like. It was clear that Brad thought he had some kind of special privilege at work, just because we hung out on the weekends. Within a few months, I had to remind him again, and this time in no uncertain terms, that this behavior, and these expectations, have to stop immediately.

This was my problem and my responsibility to manage. When it became clear that Brad couldn't separate work-Nolan from friend-Nolan, I was left with no choice but to help him move on. I did it Candidly and Respectfully, and we remained friends. But I would never hire him to work for me again.

This does not mean you can't have any friends at all at work. You will likely form close bonds with your executive team. Still, be professional about it. You're still the leader. Treat them equally, don't play favorites, and never forget your role in the company and your responsibility to the people who work there.

CONNECT THE RIGHT WAY

Create boundaries, but don't be distant. Be a human being who's running a business with the best intentions for the success of the company and its staff. Be warm, engaging, and genuinely interested in your people. You can be friendly without being everyone's friend. Get to know your staff and spend work time with each team, and with each person individually, as long as their numbers make that possible. I still connect with every person at my company on a one-to-one basis to learn about their professional goals and where they see themselves in the future with my company, or somewhere else.

Set the tone from the start with each new hire. During a person's first week, take them out to lunch or coffee, but not to chat about sports. Remember, you're not there to make friends but to have a meaningful conversation about what you and the company are trying to accomplish. Ask about the skills they want to develop and what they want to achieve in their career. Discuss how their goals and the company's might align.

Several times a year, schedule a thirty-minute conversation with the person to reinforce the tone you set at the beginning. Check in on how their goals and the company's might have changed, and whether they are still aligned. Also ask, "How are things going? Are you getting what you need from us? Are you building technical skills you wanted to get when you started here?" Be friendly but keep the focus on business.

With more than fifty people, it becomes difficult for

one leader to find the time to do regular one-on-ones with everybody. You might have to delegate them to your executive leadership team and train them to conduct those conversations effectively. Despite how big your company gets, or how busy you get, continue to stay visible and connected to your people.

When the 2020 pandemic hit and everyone had to work from home, I did one-on-ones with every staff member remotely. Due to the unique circumstances, I felt it was especially important to connect with people and assure them that we were still in business. I hadn't abandoned them, or the ship, and I still needed them to keep us afloat. Their fearless leader wasn't sitting at home all day playing video games, watching TV, and "raking in the money" they were earning for the business. I was still their leader.

If you hire your friends, you'll regret it. Years after I made those mistakes, I'm still reflecting on their impacts on my company's growth, my friends' professional growth, and on all the other staff members who were affected.

The relationships you have with the people at work—

business partners, executives, and staff—affect the entire company. For better or worse, they create a culture. A business's culture is another one of those things I was oblivious to as a young CEO. I didn't understand it, didn't know how critically important it was. Culture is the heart of the business, and just like a real heart, it pumps the fuel that keeps a company alive, moving it forward.

Culture is who you really are as a company, as you'll see in the next chapter.

QUESTIONS, ACTIONS, AND RESOURCES

Hiring people, managing them, and being the leader that they and your business need isn't intuitive, and you owe it to yourself to learn best practices and avoid the most common mistakes. Whether you're considering candidates to hire or currently dealing with staff, take a moment to answer these questions, then take action. Read more on the subject from my selection of books, below.

QUESTIONS

1. If you're thinking of hiring your friends, ask

yourself why you want them working for you. Are they true business colleagues, with greater and differentiated skills and thought patterns from yourself?

2. What conversations do you need to have with your colleagues to ensure they understand that friendship doesn't replace Accountability?

3. Be brutally honest with yourself. Do you have team members that fall in the friendship zone, and are treated differently by the rest of your staff, consciously or subconsciously?

ACTIONS

1. Identify whether you've already traded Accountability for friendship with any of your staff. Schedule a time to sit down and have the "hard talk" about what's needed for the business and how you can still maintain your friendship if the working relationship needs to change.

2. Build what the Entrepreneurial Operating System® refers to as "Accountability charts" based on roles, not names. Is your staff meeting those accountabilities? Use this chart to have the more difficult discussions where you need

to reset your Accountability expectations for your team.

3. Set up professional, one-to-one weekly meetings with your direct reports, and regardless of your personal connection, keep them focused on the business, outcomes, and Accountability.

RESOURCES

- Kim Scott, *Radical Candor (Be a Kick-Ass Boss Without Losing Your Humanity)* (London: Pan Macmillan, 2019).
- Jack Welch, *Winning* (New York: HarperCollins, 2005).
- Gino Wickman, *Traction: Get a Grip on Your Business* (Dallas: BenBella, 2011).

CULTURE

During my company's first six years, my only exposure to culture was a boring session on the subject at a minor conference. Culture seemed like so much marketing fluff—nothing I could use to improve or grow my organization. Not surprisingly, I was also pretty blasé about the need for an HR department. We were grown adults, after all. A bunch of engineers. We didn't need someone telling us how to behave; we should be mature enough to self-manage.

Any "people problems" that arose, I could handle myself. You know, like those caused by someone bringing in the wrong partner, or hiring friends, or—as the business grew—playing favorites with the old crew. Like promoting a friend who didn't really want it and wasn't qualified for the job, then demoting said friend but paying him more than other staff in the same position. Or relying on an employee/friend for all the dirt on company gossip. Or trying to run the business remotely while working two other jobs. Those kinds of problems.

I truly believed I was the expert and that everything I did turned to gold. Yes, six years in, and after all that, I still believed my own bullshit.

It wasn't like I ignored culture altogether. We had a mission statement. Whoop-de-doo. But we didn't have a functional vision statement—I didn't even know what that meant. We didn't have clear core values either. I didn't really have clarity of my own core values either, at least none that I had defined and committed to living.

A few years in, I took a stab at creating something I called "value statements." This was a list of crap like "We respond to email on time," and "Everyone gets a certification every year." Really? We're a multimillion-dollar business and we have to remind ourselves to answer email? Were we so pathetically negligent in our typical email response time that we had to create a value statement for it? I can see myself now, addressing my people: "This is what we stand for. This is who we are. We respond to emails in a timely manner. Rah-rah! Who's with me?" I never did that, but maybe I should have. It would have shown me how empty these value statements were. They had nothing to do with actual values.

Values are who you are at your core. They guide your conscience and your decisions. They're like guardrails that prevent you from making bad choices. Values point you in the right direction. They're especially critical when the path is rocky and the destination uncertain.

If I were gauging people's success by how closely they adhered to the company's "values," everyone who answered their email and got a certification would get a gold star. It didn't matter whether they told the truth, or billed their time honestly, or treated their colleagues with respect.

My lack of knowledge of business culture gave me a pass when I made bad decisions. There was no litmus test for holding myself Accountable. The impact on my staff and the business slowly caught up with me, though, and over time the effects began to show. My staff wasn't happy. Then, good people began leaving.

Everything came to a head around the end of 2017. My partner was killing the business. I was away in California, working hundred-hour weeks, killing myself. My staff was hanging in there for the most part, but probably fantasizing about doing me in—if I ever hung around long enough for them to find me. The company's culture was in the crapper. I didn't realize this of course, because I still didn't understand culture or how it affects a business. All I knew was that my company was in trouble, and I didn't know what to do about it. I had no direction, no guiding light, no principles to inform my decisions and put me back on track. No *values*.

I took a sabbatical. For two months (I had planned three, but my partner was doing some extra torpedoing while I was out), I stepped away from the business to take care of myself. During that time, I actually got a therapist to help me get myself back on track. If you've been following along, you're probably wondering how a guy like me—a guy who thought he knew everything, who launched his own business at twenty-three and took no one's advice but his own—could bring himself to get help. On my own, I never would have. My girlfriend talked me into it. She's now my fiancée.

Getting that help was exactly what I needed. The therapist helped me see what I was doing wrong and why, and how to make it right. She taught me to value myself and to treat myself the way I deserved to be treated. When I came back to work and had to face all the company's problems head-on, it only made sense to apply that same strategy to my business. I needed to get clarity on what I valued most in my company and come up with a plan to run it the way it deserved to be run.

I needed professional help of another kind. So I hired a business coach.

Roger had a lot of experience with companies the same size as Intrinium. He'd seen them suffer the same issues. I hired him to coach my leadership team—myself and my partner Stewart included—for what I described as communication problems.

It didn't take long for Roger to figure out that our culture was in trouble. And fixing it had to come from the top, from the owners. I clearly remember a month or so after starting with Roger, he brought Stewart and me into his office for an offsite meeting and clearly stated, "There is a power struggle, and you guys need to get right between each other." Stewart immediately replied, "Oh no, Nolan and I are good. We don't have any communication problems; we just want you to teach our mid-level managers how to manage."

Roger and I moved forward without him.

VALUES ARE JUST THAT: WHAT YOU *VALUE*

Intrinium's culture was falling apart. There was at least one counterculture, maybe more—people so fed up, they were actively working *against* the company's goals. We had no boundaries and no structure for communicating with each other. People had different ideas on what we were trying to accomplish and who we should be selling to. The only rule that seemed clear to everyone was that no one was allowed to disagree with Stewart. It was basically his way or the highway. So instead of arguing with him, they did whatever they wanted and just didn't discuss it.

You can't change a bad culture by working around the edges. That's like peeling the brown spots off an apple that's rotten to the core. To change the way people communicate, behave, make decisions, and treat each other, you have to start with removing the rot from the core. At that core are values: literally, what you *value* most as a company. This is not about emails or certifications. It's what matters to you—the business leader and your staff—that shape the way your business operates.

With values, I would have a touchstone for making decisions. This part is super important, because though companies do a good job creating a mission statement and vision statement, their values often suck. It's as if they googled "value statement" and grabbed the first thing that came up. Values are personal. Even though they apply to your company, if you want your values to shape the culture in a positive way, they have to be ideals that you believe in and either currently live by or aspire to uphold. You have to believe in them enough to commit to running your business by them.

Our values would have to stand the test of time, so we could look to them now and ten years from now. They would have to be valid at our current size and in the future, no matter how much we grew. Our values couldn't be goal-oriented because goals change. I spent months thinking about what Intrinium's values should be. I'd close my office door and think, research, and write. I'd meet with people in the company and bounce ideas off them. Finally, I had our values.

VALUES DEFINE THE MORAL STRUCTURE OF A BUSINESS

I refer to Intrinium's values as "pillars." Like sturdy columns that form the structure of a building, our pillars form the moral structure of the business. They make evident who we are and what we stand for. They also drive our behavior, actions, and decisions.

Pillar #1, Integrity: Integrity matters in any industry. In security, it's especially important because we are protecting other companies' most critical information and data. For our customers to trust us, we need to be able to trust each other.

Pillar #2, Accountability: We need to own every

commitment, internal or external, and see it through to completion. Accountability doesn't imply perfection; it means taking responsibility, learning from failures, and doing better the next time.

Pillar #3, Proactive Communication: This is about letting other people know when a commitment is going sideways so we have an opportunity to do something about it. Waiting until it's too late or trying to cover up a failure does not model Integrity or Accountability, and only serves to exacerbate the problem. Keeping problems hidden erodes trust. Like the other pillars, Proactive Communication extends to customer interactions. Occasionally things go wrong, but they go a lot less wrong with Proactive Communication.

Pillar #4, Respectful Candor: Say what you mean. Don't beat around the bush. Don't be a jerk, but don't refrain from important conversations simply to spare someone's feelings. Respectful Candor is clear and addresses the problem; it does not attack the person. Mutual respect among employees promotes lifting other people up to be, and do, their best—it does not seek to tear people down.

Pillar #5, Growth Mindset: Particularly in tech where skills become obsolete within years—sometimes months—continuous learning is a requirement. Customers expect a company like ours to be cutting edge, prepared to leverage new technologies, and take on the latest threats. We are always looking for ways to innovate and improve.

VALUES ARE GUIDES

Although pillars guide how we make business decisions, they are not restrictions. With the exception of the Integrity pillar, they're also not prescriptions. They ensure healthy interaction without limiting anyone's thought process. The Growth Mindset pillar is an example. People learn things in different ways, and I don't always expect my staff to take a specified training. What's more important is that they continue to learn, through whatever means, and around whatever topics make sense for them and their role. When the learning path is clear, the person follows it.

For example, our service-desk techs require key certifications, so their learning follows that path. An operations leader might study books on leadership and clear communication to further their education on those topics, while a director of finance might get an advanced degree or pursue financial certifications that prepare them for a CFO role. The choice of learning depends on their current education, experience, and skills, what they need to improve for their role or a future role, and their preferred learning materials and methods. Values are like guardrails that set strong boundaries—they're not handcuffs.

VALUES EMPOWER EMPLOYEES AND FREE UP LEADERS

Values empower employees to make decisions on their own without worrying whether it's the right call. This not only builds confidence and character in your staff, but it also allows them to get their jobs done without having to check in with their leadership on every single decision. This frees up time for you and your executive team to focus on strategies for improving and growing the business.

It's like the African proverb "It takes a village." Everyone is responsible for enabling each other person to reach their full potential. Likewise, they're all responsible for keeping each other in line. The rules of the village—the values or pillars—are established and everyone agrees to abide by them. When someone is operating outside those boundaries, it's apparent. Strong values create a self-regulating mechanism. People perform within the culture, or they self-select out of it. With a strong culture, you rarely have to fire anyone, and if you do, they know it's coming. There are no surprises.

INDIVIDUALS ALIGN TO CULTURE...OR THEY DON'T

Having a mission statement makes clear what you are trying to accomplish to the highest standard, in the present. In the simplest form, it explains what your company does. A vision statement looks to the future. But without values, there are no rules for how you accomplish either.

Culture is those rules. Culture drives people to work toward a shared purpose in a healthy way that motivates them to want what you want because ultimately, they want it to. They aren't just signing on for a paycheck—they want themselves, their colleagues, and the company to succeed. Of course, this means that not everyone will conform to your culture. People may flat out just not be a good fit.

If this is the case, they will figure that out soon enough and opt out of the company. They'll leave.

That's exactly what happened at Intrinium. Once we had established our pillars and communicated them to the staff, people were aware of how we adhered to them. They were also aware of when we did not.

Culture sets you apart. Every person can add value to a business, but not everyone can add value to every business. If a person's values do not align with a company's culture, they will struggle to add value. Defining your values and building a culture around them creates a common language. A healthy culture obliterates ulterior motives and vague expectations. It's the filter through which you view the people and the decisions that drive your organization. That filter also repels people who don't share your company's values. This isn't a judgment on those people's characters—companies and people have different values, and sometimes a person isn't a good fit. However, they may be a perfect fit somewhere else.

ESTABLISHING THE RIGHT CULTURE

Whether or not you realize it, your company already has a culture. People brought part of it with them. You helped define it too, and you reinforce it with your actions, decisions, and responses to other people's actions and decisions.

Unless you intentionally figure out what kind of culture you want and can believe in, and make an effort to communicate it and commit to it, you will end up with one that doesn't reflect what you want the company to be.

You're welcome to adopt my company's value pillars, though you probably have some ideas of your own. As you define your values, make sure they apply to any problems you foresee, and any decisions that must be made. Your values should be such that anyone in your company can apply them to their work. They should be clear, easy to explain, and applicable this year, next year, and ten years from now.

You may want to revisit your mission statement and vision statement too. Though these items don't necessarily define culture, they are impacted by it.

CULTURE AND DIVERSITY

Your organizational culture does not preclude diversity. In fact, the opposite is true: it demands it. Your customers don't all look, act, and think alike. They vary in age, gender, race, religion, and sexual orientation. Some have formal educations while others gained skills through experiential learning. Your staff will be better prepared to understand your customer base if they reflect it. The more diverse, the better, because each person brings different background, experiences, and worldview to the picture that enrich your culture, making it deeper, stronger, and more current with changing times.

My company sits in a county with limited ethnic diversity, which challenges our ability to attract diverse talent. Still, our employees—including the leadership team—represent a spectrum of people who may not all look the same, yet we share the same Intrinium values. Those pillars not only hold the company up, but they also allow us to hold our heads up and proudly say, "This is who we are—all of us."

When we recruit new people, we vet candidates based on their qualifications and their values. Can you imagine a business where everyone came from the same place, had identical experiences, and they all thought alike? That would seriously limit the opportunities for innovation. Incorporating diversity makes the company better; because everyone is different, we can all learn from each other.

So, when I talk about looking for people who share our values, I'm not focused on their color, gender, age, or physical condition. I'm looking for Integrity and Proactive Communication. I want to know how the person feels about Accountability and Respectful Candor. And I want to know whether they have a passion for learning, or if they think they know everything there is to know. If they meet those criteria, those values, they are strong candidates. They also need to be qualified for the position, but no matter how qualified they are, if they don't support our pillars, they won't get the job.

Without our pillars, it would be difficult to achieve our mission and vision. Defining your approach, how you interact with each other and with customers, is imperative for growth. Trying to scale the business beyond your initial circle of employees and maintain culture isn't possible unless you first define it and communicate it to everyone—even those people you don't interact with every day, or ever. Without that, people's decisions are going to be based on whatever values they brought into the business.

A mission, vision, and *especially* values have to be far more than words on your website that you show your customers. Don't confuse them with marketing. You can make them public, but they are intended for your people. Their purpose is to hold leaders and employees accountable to each other and to guide every decision made.

If you're looking for a ready-made framework for this process, we found that the Entrepreneurial Operating System (EOS) championed by Gino Wickman in his book *Traction*, which I recommended in Chapter 4's "Resources," has a clearly defined path for identifying and communicating these concepts.

YOU MIGHT NEED A COACH

You can start the work on your culture alone and then bring in your executive team to help. But if you have a situation like mine where your partner or you yourself are part of the culture problem, you may need a coach. Having a third party to guide the process can help eliminate conflict.

Without a coach, you and your partner could end up going at it—with your employees losing faith in you and your ability to lead. A business coach who understands culture problems and solutions can step you through the process and help you communicate it properly to your staff. They can show you things you won't notice on your own, either due to inexperience, or because you've been looking at them so long, you stopped noticing.

A coach is also not emotionally attached to the business, so they are more objective. By the time I hired Roger, I was feeling anger, grief, despair, and frustration with myself, my partner, and my staff. And I'm not an emotional person. I just wanted to get past all those feelings and get the company back on track. To do that, I had to set my emotions aside. Our coach showed me how to do that, correcting me when I was wrong, and encouraging me when I was getting it right. Roger had my best interests and those of the company at heart, so there was no worry about his motivations. I could trust him.

COMMUNICATING CULTURAL EXPECTATIONS ON DAY 1

When an employee joins a company, they bring the baggage of every place they've worked before. Whatever culture they experienced is coming with them to your business. If that culture was great, well so much the better. But if it were truly great, would they have left that company to begin with? More often, it's all the bad stuff that made them want to leave.

People don't do this intentionally. Culture becomes ingrained in us, especially when we're working in the thick of it five days a week for eight, nine, ten hours a day. Without even realizing it, we can get sucked into the gossip, avoiding telling all the truth all the time, or not always doing what's best for the customer. This is why you have to have the culture conversation with people during the hiring process and repeat it during onboarding. Refer to it in meetings and during important decisions. Remind people regularly how you, they, and the business operate. This starts during the interview process, is reinforced during onboarding via training materials and recommended reading, and is referred back to regularly in the work.

It's not enough to throw your values up on a slide or a whiteboard. You have to show people how those values can be applied by them in their specific roles. For example, at Intrinium, almost every newcomer struggles with the pillar "Respectful Candor." They're so used to keeping their heads down and holding comments to themselves, that they're uncomfortable speaking out, especially to someone in a higher role. New people need a tutorial on this concept, so they understand that to align with our values, they are not only allowed to speak up—we expect it! They need to understand that they're not going to be chastised for correcting their colleagues or leadership, including me. We literally have to give them examples, or they just agree to the values and never practice them.

MAINTAINING CULTURE VIGILANCE

Like every lesson in this book, I didn't get it 100

percent right the first time. Even after all the culture work, the inevitable happened: I got busy, we got busy, and the culture suffered. We had a lot of new contracts to satisfy, and doubling our staff within four months brought an influx of talent from other companies. I let my guard down about conveying cultural expectations, thinking it wasn't as high a priority as getting the work done. *I'll get to it later, when we're caught up,* I told myself; *the culture is strong.*

Within nine months, that mistake earned me two groups of staff: those who bought into the culture, and the new hires who had retained their "us versus them, management is out to get us" mentality. That counterculture of fear and passive-aggressiveness bled through the ranks, creating drama that left us struggling to hit what would normally be an easy target: billing 80 percent of our time. We couldn't meet our commitments to our customers because we were basically paying people to sit around, bitch, and plot revenge on their managers. There was an internal war going on, and imagined or not, it was using up resources that we couldn't spare.

In a bigger company, countercultures are common

and often go unnoticed because the players make up a smaller percentage of the staff. But in a company of fifty people or so, every individual counts, and they'd better all be playing for your team. Even one bad actor can have a dramatic impact on the culture.

When you're in a leadership role, assume that the first time you hear about something, it's the hundredth time it's happened. Once again, I missed the red flags (are you noticing a pattern?) and by the time the bad actors came to my attention, their influence had already begun to eat away at the values we'd cultivated. It's true that what you allow, you support. Because I didn't act immediately, the culture decay had festered and spread, and I had to release several people who may have been able to work out well with proper onboarding. Or rather, I "freed up their futures" for new jobs. These weren't awful people; they just could not find alignment with Intrinium's values. After they left, the consensus among the staff was, "We loved those people—we just didn't love working with them."

No one is immune to the need to embrace culture—not the executive in the corner office, or the person who sweeps the floors, and certainly not the individual who brings in the most money. I don't care how great they are at their job or how valuable they are to the business. The person who can do the most damage is the guy who believes the rules don't apply to him, the guy who thinks *you need me, you can't fire me, so I can do whatever I want.* If you let that superstar hold you hostage, you'll end up with a bunch of high-performing jerks who can't get along with anyone and are all about themselves, not about the business. They'll infect other people too, leading them to ask *why am I killing myself to do the right thing when only jackasses are rewarded around here?*

As Jack Welch wrote in his book *Winning*, you have to make a public example of that kind of person. Fire them and let the staff know that it's not enough to be a star performer; they also have to meet the company's cultural requirements. That's the only way to reinforce your team's positive values.

REDUCING THE ENVIRONMENTAL FALLOUT

The absence or presence of values affects more than

decisions. It affects the entire atmosphere and how people feel when they come to work in the morning. Before establishing our pillars, our employee surveys showed mediocre levels of job satisfaction. In particular, the executive management team was frustrated because they felt like they were herding cats. There was no structure in place that said, "This is how we do things around here."

Our value pillars gave the business that ethical structure, and just as structural pillars raise a roof, our pillars also raised job satisfaction. For the first time in a long time, people enjoyed their work because they knew how decisions were being made. The pillars eliminated fear and uncertainty. Employees understood what we were trying to accomplish, versus being pressured to hit revenue goals. We were all on the same team, supporting one another toward the same goals, with mutual respect and trust.

The transformation didn't happen overnight. It took time, and it took removing people who didn't want to get on board. Of course, there was plenty of blowback every time someone was let go due to being unable to strive for our pillars. People worried that they were going to be next, so we had to explain that what we were doing was for the good of the company—for the good of everyone who remained.

If changes happen in secret, people tend to make up their own reasons, their own story, which is always worse than reality. You have to control the narrative by being the first one out front with the *real* story. Emphasizing why we were making these tough decisions helped people realize we weren't only talking about values; we were *living* them. We didn't terminate anyone for personal reasons—there were valid reasons, and if they understood the importance of our values, they would see why we had no other choice. After two high-profile people were let go, in the practice of *Candor*, I held a town hall to explain the decision. This wasn't about trashing people. I was Respectful, but I made it clear that no matter how good, how nice, or how valuable a person is, unless they live up to our pillars, there is no place for them here.

Even after the town hall, I had to keep up my vigilance. Amid change, people immediately default to fear, so even though my staff heard my words, they didn't automatically believe me. I had to continue proving to them over and over that I meant what I said: Our values matter. Our pillars are critical. We stand by them and support them because they are what holds us up as a different kind of company.

Other people were let go, and some were very popular among the staff. Some received generous severance packages.

We weren't crucifying people. We still respected them. But if we didn't prioritize our values and live up to them, they meant nothing. A person was let go for one reason and one reason only: they had violated one of the pillars—had many opportunities to get on track and just couldn't do it.

Leadership is about transparent communications between the leader and the team. By that, I don't just mean showing them everything that's going on. You have to over-communicate your goals and the reasons behind them. You also have to create an environment in which your team members feel free to share their career goals. This isn't just one conversation you have with each employee. It's a continuous process because people change, and if you're doing things right, their levels of trust and Candor will grow. As you maintain and further deepen your communication, you'll find that, with trust and understanding established, the team you're leading will become more than "extra hands"—they'll be motivated to lead the real efforts required to achieve the vision you've carefully drawn and communicated because they understand it and are as excited as you are to achieve them.

Conversely, if you don't keep up the conversation, the trust and Candor subside. The channels of communication dissolve. Trust is essential for working toward aligning everyone's goals. This is the opposite of management by carrot-and-stick incentives, moving targets, or any other form of manipulation. Those strategies are more likely to get people to leave.

IF I HAD TO DO IT ALL OVER AGAIN

If my twenty-three-year-old self stepped into my office today and said he was starting a business, I'd have an earful to tell him. We'd spend a whole day—maybe a whole week—on culture. Granted, he'd make a run for the door, but I'd make him listen because I wouldn't want him, or any business owner, to learn about culture the hard way. Here's what I would tell that guy:

Never underestimate the value of the effort you put into optimizing your company's culture. It will pay off in the long run. It's your job as founder, owner, leader, or CEO to sort this out. Do not hand it off to HR or any other department. Put in the work. Tackling culture when I first started my business would have saved me the emotional turmoil and financial cost of letting go 5 percent, maybe even 10 percent of my staff over the years. Knowing what I know now, I would make that trade in a heartbeat.

First, define your mission and vision. Figure out what you want your company to do and put it in writing. Many books and web resources cover those topics in detail, so I'm not focusing on them here.

Then define your values. This step deserves—*demands*—a lot of time to think things through on your own. Write down guidelines for how to deal with all the challenges you face in business: deciding what services to offer, which clients to go after, how to communicate with colleagues, staff, and management; how to make staffing decisions; and how to make any other day-to-day decisions. Start big and broad so you're covering all the scenarios. My first list included about thirty ideas and none made the final cut. But this is how you start to think about the ways your values will guide your work, interactions, and decisions in a practical way.

I did a lot of reading too, and I looked up the values of companies I respected, such as Apple, Amazon, Google, and my major competitors. We were different than those companies. Not different in a bad way, but unique in our own, good way. I had to think about what made us different. How was Intrinium different in the best way possible? When was I most proud of my company, my leadership, my people? These thoughts showed me what we did right, what I wanted us to do more of. These were the values that set us apart.

I wrote down my ideas, and instead of sharing them immediately, I set them aside. That was hard, because as much as I wanted to show everyone my "accomplishment," I first needed to test them. I set my values—my pillars—aside for a few weeks, and whenever a business challenge arose, I referred to them to see whether they made sense.

I strongly urge you to follow this advice. Until you test your values, you won't know whether they work for your organization, or cover the many challenges and decisions you deal with as the leader of a company. Once you're confident that they work, communicate them to everyone else.

You may spend a whole day figuring out how to clearly communicate just one value. This kind of thinking is real work. It can be exhausting. If you've spent hours figuring out the best way to explain your company's new values and you feel like you're wasting your time, you're not. It can take that long to get it right. Get some coffee or whatever you drink, close your door, and figure it out.

INTRODUCE THE CULTURE AND GET BUY-IN

Kick-off your new culture with an all-staff meeting. Walk the staff through your decision to rework your mission, vision, and values, and your expectations about applying them. Once you've communicated them, let people know that they are not going to be held accountable for them until the rollout is complete. We actually spent three or four weeks talking about what each pillar means and how to apply them.

Don't expect everyone to love your ideas right away. You can't just issue an edict and expect everyone to fall in line. Getting buy-in takes time, and the bigger the staff, the longer it could take. With say, fifty people or more, you'll want to implement a formal process. Your executives, managers, and HR people will need to accept your proposal and build the values into their processes.

Encourage collaboration. Ask your leadership team to come up with their own ideas for communicating and implementing your company's values. I gave the managers six weeks to come up with their plan. That timeframe was reasonable because the project was added to their typical workload, but also because they needed time to understand our values, which we were calling pillars. If they didn't, they would not have been able to teach them to everyone else. The managers came back with a workable plan that they owned. It included incorporating the pillars into people's performance-improvement plans.

IMPLEMENT THE CULTURE... SLOWLY

Call me cynical, but I believe that only about half of what you communicate at the executive level makes it from execs to managers to individual contributors. Leadership may get tired of the word "values," but you have to repeat yourself, so it reaches everyone in the organization.

For the first six months, we were still having conversations to set expectations and let people know this values thing wasn't going away. When something went wrong, I would say, "Let's see how that stacks up against our pillars. Did we do it the Intrinium way? No? Then what can we do differently next time?" The process never ends because you need to keep reinforcing it or people will fall back to doing what's most comfortable or convenient.

Six months in, I noticed the conversations really begin to change. People were talking about our pillars without me having to bring them up. They were referring to them to solve problems, defend their actions, and make decisions.

Several steps in this process helped make our culture transformation a success. Before you introduce a new (or your first) mission, vision, and values, I recommend including them in your culture plan.

Get a Coach

So much was riding on the new pillar rollout that I didn't try to do it alone. Roger, our business coach, worked with our executive and management teams on applying the new pillars to our processes, including hiring.

Evaluate New Employees

Whenever we interview anyone, we evaluate them by their capabilities, but we also add questions related to our pillars. We want people who can grow with the company. We want people with Integrity who are able to speak their minds too. A candidate might check all the boxes in the skills categories, but if they can't participate in Respectful, Candid conversation, they won't fit in with our culture. In some cases, we realize these skills can be developed and improved if the person is willing, and we take that into consideration in our hiring decision.

Provide Informal Rewards

The managers came up with an idea that really caught on and allowed everyone to get involved. Any staff member can nominate another one for an award for demonstrating one of the pillars. Then, at our monthly town halls, we honor the winners. It's a fun way to raise awareness and integrate the pillars into the culture throughout the organization. This informal reward system gives people ownership of the values and allows them to connect them to their work, instead of the pillars being seen as simply "high ideals" that the company has thrust upon them. Each individual owns the pillars and models them within their roles in their own way.

Include Values in Formal Reviews

We also use the pillars in performance evaluations, where managers assess their staffs and vice versa. We use what's called the Entrepreneurial Operating System, mentioned earlier, which is a set of processes for which people earn a plus or minus for each pillar, or culture category.

Hold Each Other Accountable

People with two or more minuses are invited to a conversation where we talk about the pillars, why they matter to the organization, and what the person can do to better fulfill them. Sometimes it's just a matter of a tier-one service desk person being reluctant to candidly tell their manager that they're wrong about something. I remind the individual that being Respectfully Candid is part of the job and reassure them that they will not be punished for it. These conversations don't set a person up for firing, and I let them know that too. They're an opportunity to improve so they and the company can do better.

Accountability is the most challenging pillar to implement and maintain. People who resist this value often have a scarcity—not a growth—mindset. If they see Accountability as something that will be used against them instead of a way for everyone to be successful, they're unlikely to ever be a good fit. This goes both ways: people have to be open to being held accountable and willing to speak up and hold others accountable, but always with Respectful Candor and in the best interests of the person and the company.

If a staff member is a good performer yet cannot accept Accountability, their manager might be reluctant to enforce the Accountability pillar. Sure, it sucks to call out your star performer, but you have to do it. No one person is above the culture. No one is immune to the values you've all agreed to uphold. The CEO's role in this is to make sure everyone sticks to your culture values, or you'll see a steady erosion and lose all credibility.

SET CULTURE, OR CULTURE WILL SET ITSELF

Better than most, I know the importance of culture because I did it all so wrong the first time. Ignoring culture led to anxiety and chaos. There was a lack of trust, of certainty, of optimism, or of excitement. No one ever really knew where we were going as a company and whether their jobs were safe. Six months after implementing our framework for how we work and how we make decisions, the anxiety levels dropped for me and for all the staff.

A strong and healthy culture is a business differentiator. More than anything else, it enables your business to thrive, especially over the long term. It gets you out of the taskmaster mindset of having to make every single decision. It reduces your and everyone else's stress levels while ensuring your business is what you want it to be. And it attracts and retains clients because they get consistent treatment from your company as opposed to "however your staff member happens to feel that day."

You'll attract the staff you want, too, and they'll be happy to work for you. A values-driven culture changes the environment, bringing meaning and purpose to the work. Employees know they are showing up every day for more than a paycheck. They are part of something they believe in. The attitude filters through to customers too. You end up with better and more loyal ones because they enjoy working with you and your team. An unexpected benefit from our culture transformation was the emails I received from long-time customers who noticed the positive change. And it just got better and better.

VALIDATION

Coming back from sabbatical, I didn't know where my company was headed. I wondered whether being a business owner was even worth all the hard work and disappointment. But after managing our culture problem, my business not only recovered, it came back better than ever. We started hitting our revenue goals every quarter, then we blew them out of the water.

We came out strong enough to operate through curveballs like COVID-19, the pandemic's impact on healthcare (one of our major markets), and the financial fallout. Thanks to all the work we did on our culture, our executive and management teams communicate better. We know what we stand for and we are all in it together. The business has a new image and a new attitude. It's a cool place to work—so cool, we won Best Place to Work in the Inland Northwest. The first award came six months into the definition of our culture, as a result of all the work our team did around that subject. Over the following two years, we won the award two more times, both after Stewart left and during COVID-19—periods when navigating and maintaining culture came with some difficult challenges.

You can master every lesson in this book and get great results, but none of that insulates you from failure. In fact, as you'll see in the next chapter, you should not even try to avoid failure. A healthy culture sets you up for success, but maybe even more important, it helps you deal with failure too.

QUESTIONS, ACTIONS, AND RESOURCES

When you're running a business, trying to hit financial goals, stay on top of industry trends, and deal with colleagues, customers, and staff, culture isn't exactly top of mind. But unless you make it a priority and intentionally work to establish a culture you believe in, and that works for your business, a culture will develop on its own, and it may not be the kind of culture that's beneficial to you, your people, or your company. Get ahead of it by establishing and cultivating the right culture. Here are some questions to ask yourself, actions you can take, and resources to help you avoid the mistakes that I made and get your company culture right.

QUESTIONS

1. Do you feel like you need to be involved in the minutiae of every single decision to maintain consistency in your business? You are likely missing a clearly defined set of values or pillars

for your team to use as a foundation for those decisions.

2. What kind of coach should you hire to support you? Business, life, or both?

3. Do you, as the top of the pyramid in your business, radiate the culture your business must live to be successful?

ACTIONS

1. Take a shot at defining your values. Don't overthink it. I suggest taking a perspective of "When things go wrong, who will we be?" Write down ten, fifteen, or twenty different ideals, behaviors, or principles, and let them simmer for a while, refining the list down to a handful of easy-to-remember values that define how your team will interact with each other and your customers (internal or external).

2. Hire a coach. Seriously. Google-search coaches in your area or nearby areas, interview a few, and hire one. It'll be one of the best decisions you'll ever make.

3. Re-envision your role. You aren't the CEO or Founder anymore. You're the Chief Pillars Officer, and your job isn't to solve all of the

problems, it's to teach everyone around you how to solve problems while relying on your core values.

RESOURCES

- Ori Brafman and Rom Brafman, *Sway: The Irresistible Pull of Irrational Behavior* (New York: Doubleday Random House, 2008).
- Carol S. Dweck, *Mindset: The New Psychology of Success* (New York: Penguin Random House, 2016).

FAILURE

There's no such thing as being perfect in business. Failure happens. It might happen because you're experimenting—the best possible reason. It could also happen due to inexperience (guilty), hubris (guilty), greed (guilty), or because of an inability or refusal to learn from one's mistakes (oh so very, very guilty).

Early on at Intrinium, I signed a large account. The client was located in a rural area with a shallow talent pool, and they needed an IT manager, so we placed one of our people at their site full time to handle the job. To maximize our profits, and because we couldn't afford much else (we were four people at the time), we sent an entry-level person.

The training we provided before dispatching this poor guy to the customer site consisted of "This is how they've always done the job, this is how many hours we want you to work, and oh—you also need to manage the client's politics." *Because we trust you, new guy, to single-handedly manage our newest, biggest account.*

Within a few months, the IT person and the customer were complaining about each other. My guy said the customer treated him like crap. The client said my guy couldn't do the job. I chalked it up to a personality clash and sent a *new* entry-level guy over—with the same training. That person screwed up the account so egregiously that I had to fire him. Halfway through the three-year contract, I tried a third person. My only extra advice was, "Don't repeat the other two guys' mistakes."

You can imagine how that turned out. My guy wasn't happy, and by this time, the customer was beyond frustrated with my company. Again and again and again, we weren't taking care of business for them. Three times we sent them a person who wasn't qualified to do the job. It shouldn't have gone that far. The first mistake can almost be forgiven as a genuine error in judgment, but the second? The third?

So naturally, I fired the customer. You read that right. Yes, I fired them, because I thought *they* were the problem—their culture and politics made it impossible for my people to succeed.

Yet the entire time, *we* were the problem. Regardless of any issues our client had, our company culture was so out of whack we couldn't see our own mistakes. Even if we had, we wouldn't have owned them. We had no defined values, no pillars, and no principles for how we carried ourselves. We had no rules for making decisions or interacting with clients. I wasn't the role model my people deserved. I wasn't setting the standard or providing the training they needed to succeed.

Even though that experience happened many years ago, it still haunts me. It's embarrassing now to put it in writing as a confession to the world. Most of my current staff and colleagues have never seen that side of me. Today, "Accountability" is my middle name.

Without Accountability, you are nobody. You stand for nothing.

That concept didn't occur to me until much later—too late to save that account. But I hope the lesson serves as a warning to whoever reads this book. When you screw up, admit it. Own it. Don't look for someone to blame. Figure out how to fix it and don't make the same stupid mistake twice. Or in my case, three times.

SUCCESS AND FAILURE AREN'T THAT FAR APART

People often make the mistake of seeing success and failure as mutually exclusive outcomes. If you don't win, you're a loser. Techies and engineers are particularly prone to this binary way of thinking (maybe it has something to do with all those ones and zeroes), but society also reinforces the attitude. The idea that no good can come from failure (and similarly, that there is no downside to success) is drummed into us as children, bringing home passing or failing grades on our report cards.

We celebrate the successes with no regard for all the failures we may have experienced to get there. Likewise, we're ashamed of our failures, no matter how many lessons they taught us, or how much closer they brought us to eventual success.

In truth, failure and success are deeply intertwined.

THE FAILURE FALLACY

Failure's bad reputation is the gift that keeps on giving. When leaders chalk up a few missteps—which are *inevitable* in business—people who view success as an all-or-nothing proposition let those failures weigh them down. They take the outcome personally, as if not achieving a goal defines them as a failure, incapable of success. That belief makes them fearful of taking another chance, another risk, sometimes even another step.

Leading a business is undeniably hard, and you may feel like you're failing a lot more than you're winning. It may even be factually true. But dwelling on failures will inhibit your agility and your ability to respond when something major comes up, like a global pandemic.

Winning so much so early in my career left me

totally unprepared for my first failures. I thought I was too smart to stumble, too clever to crack. When I did fall on my face, I took it personally, got discouraged, and stayed in denial for far too long to respond. When things got so bad that I couldn't ignore them, escape seemed like the best option.

TREADING WATER

Some people react to failure, not by escaping, but by running in place. The reason my former partner didn't want to try to scale our business was that he had tried and failed several times to scale his independent company. He concluded it was just not possible to break out and grow to be anything more than a very small business in our town, so he pronounced himself comfortable at that level and focused on maximizing profits at any cost.

I believe a high percentage of business owners think the same way: *we've proven that we can't grow beyond this point, so let's just stay where we are and call it good enough.* The business often gets capped at a size that keeps a lot of hats on the leader's head: manager, salesperson, strategist, HR department. When my company was smaller, I was wearing so many hats that running the business felt like playing whack-a-mole.

A company can't grow beyond the threshold of scaling when just one person is the core of the company. Failure to take risks limits a company's growth. Failing to risk failure is a growth-killer. You cheat yourself out of the possibilities, and out of that shot of confidence that comes from taking a risk and—regardless of the outcome—realizing the world won't end.

FAILURE IS USUALLY QUIETER AND SMALLER THAN YOU THINK

If you're hesitant to take risks because you fear the shame that comes from your failed attempt being "found out" by the public or the industry, this might comfort you: *they probably won't even know about it.* While I was dwelling on my mistakes, the world saw only the points adding up on my scoreboard. They figured, "Hey, Nolan's still playing the game, so he must be successful."

They didn't know about all the crap going on: all the times I struck out, the nights I couldn't sleep, the worrying over my health, my staff, my mortgage.

Even my family and friends saw only the good news. Sure, I worked hard, got lucky, and the company attracted big bucks, but what they didn't know was that I fucked up constantly. But no one updates their LinkedIn profile with "Hey, guess who screwed the pooch today? This guy!" No one even tells their mom when they mess up. So unless you're making your fuckups part of the conversation at the country club or the dinner table, most people have no idea what you've been up to.

In your mind, the failure you fear is probably much, much bigger than the reality. It's human nature to build up unpredictable outcomes in our minds, but situations are seldom as bad as what your brain tells you when you're lying in bed, staring at the ceiling at three in the morning.

If someone had asked me the year before the 2020 pandemic, "What would happen if Intrinium's largest customer cut your revenues by 25 percent?" it would have felt like the apocalypse. I would've said, "That's going to hurt. We're on the Inc 5000 list, and suddenly everything will fall apart, I'll look like a fraud, and I'll have to do layoffs. Where's our pipeline going to come from?"

But as Mark Twain said, "I've had a lot of worries in my life, most of which never happened."

Deep in the pandemic, not only did we maintain the same team, we actually brought in people for new roles. Yeah, revenues were down, and I wasn't getting rich during that time, but I wasn't freaking out over the prospect of my business collapsing either. We were nimble enough to maneuver through the situation and keep ourselves on track. What seemed like an "end of the world" scenario was nothing more than a stumbling block.

FAILURE WILL ACTUALLY *DRIVE* SUCCESS IF YOU LET IT

My journey to the self-awareness that led to my personal health and well-being, and that of my company, was a long, hard path. But this is key: *I never would have reached this place without those hardships.* I would also not have had as much fun.

You might not believe this, but it's absolutely true. Most people find their greatest joy in challenging themselves, trying to do something difficult, failing a few times, and finally making it. When things go smoothly all the time, you don't get that sense of fulfillment.

During the height of COVID-19 and its effect on business, instead of getting discouraged and thinking, *Our best years are behind us,* I was thinking, *This is a shitty year, and next year could be rough, but at some point, this pandemic will end.* To be ready, we leaned in. Instead of cuts, we focused on improvements, developing our skills so when the time came, we'd be ready to ramp right back up. We could do that with confidence because we've been through so much and survived.

Learn to see failure for what it is: an indicator of opportunities for improvement. Face your mistakes, figure out where things went sideways, find out why, and come up with a plan so they don't happen again. Repeating a mistake is the only failure that's unacceptable. Because really, you know better. I didn't know better, but you've been warned.

You will learn much more from your failures than from your successes. I sure did. If I hadn't, this book would be boring as hell. Any business owner who's led a blessed career, never making a mistake, is either an underperformer or a liar. We all have our screwups; some of us give up, and some of us learn and move on. Tapping into the lessons that come from failure separates the still running from the also-rans.

When I started Intrinium, I was under a non-compete agreement with my previous employer. I had to get my own customers from scratch, which I would have done anyway. I made up to forty phone calls every single day, five days a week, for almost a year to attract business. On a good day, all but one of those calls either told me to get lost or just hung up on me. That's a lot of rejection on the way to the first yes. I learned to keep making calls, keep asking for the business. Because eventually, you do get to that one yes that keeps you in business. But not without a lot of noes—a lot of *fails*.

HOW TO TURN FAILURE INTO SUCCESS

Approach every failure as a learning opportunity. That perspective would have saved my company from firing a good client and a lot of other missteps. It also applies to failures like not hitting a goal, missing a deadline, and even experimenting with some innovation that doesn't work out as you'd expected. Occasionally, you may come across a failure that doesn't seem to offer a lesson. Fine. Don't dwell on it. Don't waste a lot of time looking for the lesson. Just don't repeat the same mistake. Then take your losses and move on.

EIGHT STEPS TO A SUCCESSFUL FAILURE

When—not *if*—you fail, you'll get a certain amount of success from it by following my Eight Steps to a Successful Failure:

1. Create and maintain a culture that makes it safe to fail. You have to allow for failure, or you'll perish as a company.
2. Avoid emotional reactions.
3. Specifically, avoid pointing fingers and attacking anyone personally. (The failure was an outcome, not a character flaw.)
4. Avoid taking the failure personally yourself.
5. Do a root cause analysis. Examine the factors that created the outcome. Objectively list a timeline of events and facts to note the gaps in a structured way.
6. Acknowledge anything that went right, too.

7. Consider what you learned from the failure and what you could have done to avoid it.
8. Ask yourself, "What's next?" Create a strategy for identifying and avoiding a similar failure in the future.

Notice that the eight steps reflect my pillars: Integrity, Accountability, Proactive Communication, Respectful Candor, Growth Mindset.

Having values to turn to are even more important when things aren't going as planned than when they are. Culture might not always prevent the failure right in front of you, but it allows you to address it in a healthy way and prevent it from recurring.

As the leader, remember that failures always come back to you. By taking responsibility, you don't give up control to forces outside yourself. You don't start resenting and replacing your staff. If people aren't measuring up, remember that you hired them, or you hired the people who hired them. Ultimately, it all comes back to you. Now it's on you to fix it.

A way to avoid emotional reactions and subjectivity is to focus on actionable solutions. If the failure happened because of stuff going on in someone's personal life, you can't do anything with that. But it is actionable to see that you needed better systems and people in place to support that person while they were tied up in personal matters. Or to realize you failed to hold the employee accountable to their goal and to candid and Proactive Communication.

After dealing with the failure and asking, "What's next?" you can either go after the same goal in the same way, or go after the same goal but by positioning yourself differently. You can add skills or resources. Or you can revise the goal to make it reachable with what you already have. Just don't leave the failure hanging out there. Take that next step.

Contrast the eight steps to the all-too-common approaches of ignoring failures or getting angry about them and shaming the people responsible. When no one looks for a solution, the failure and its aftermath are likely to repeat themselves until that person isn't just shamed, they're fired. That forces everyone else to walk around on eggshells and focus on staying out of trouble. Slap someone on the wrist enough times, and you can't expect them to take risks and innovate. They will revert to doing the minimum to stay "out of trouble."

Culture allows room to fail. If someone tries something, fails at it, and tells me about it, my first job is to make them feel safe. I'm likely to say something like this: "Thank you for demonstrating Growth Mindset (Proactive Communication, or whatever the pillar is that supports their actions). I'm sorry what you attempted didn't work out, but I love that you felt you could take this leap. What did you learn?"

FAILURE IS THE MEANS TO THE END

Success is the tip of the iceberg. Everything else is how you got there. The path to success is paved with failure.

Look at Thomas Edison and his ten thousand light bulb prototypes. Or Steve Jobs. Or Elon Musk. Most of us remember only the successes and forget how many failures these guys chalked up on the way to getting it right.

Failure is not the end. Multiple failures are not,

either. They can be the prerequisite to success. How you course-correct determines what happens after it. This book represents the tip of an iceberg. People might think I just sat down and wrote it. Unless they actually read it, like you're doing, they'll never understand the effort, challenges, failures, and pain I went through to get to a point where I had something to say.

Failure never feels good. It's never made me happy; I've never celebrated it. But I've failed enough to know that failure is worth all the pain in the long run. Rebounding from failures shows you are a leader strong enough to overcome whatever comes your way.

If, on the other hand, you find you're so afraid of failure that you won't take risks, leadership is probably not for you. In that case, I recommend that you find yourself a job with low stakes and a guaranteed paycheck. I suspect that's not you, though. You've gotten this far, and despite the challenges, you probably see the rewards, too.

As I mentioned, I would never have reached the success I enjoy today if I had not ultimately learned to recover from failure. Because failure is so often a prerequisite to success, it seems appropriate to follow up in the next chapter with one of my favorite topics: success.

QUESTIONS, ACTIONS, AND RESOURCES

A certain degree of failure is inevitable in any business. How you deal with it, what you learn from it, and what you do next determines that failure's impact, for better or worse. Here are some questions, actions, and resources to help you prepare for failure, face it, and succeed not only in spite of it, but often because of it.

QUESTIONS

1. Consider whatever event in your life you consider to be your biggest failure. What did you learn that you've applied since?
2. What's the "big thing" you've not taken a leap at yet? Be honest and ask yourself "Why?"
3. What's scarier: Having tried and failed, or looking back at your life, not having tried due to fear?

ACTIONS

1. Make a "fears list." Write down all the fears that are holding you back and stare at them honestly. Is the list truly that scary? Is there nothing you can do to mitigate the worst outcomes in advance? Are there even any truly "bad" outcomes?

2. Take the power from your fears. Tell your significant other, business partner, therapist, someone about them. When you state your fears out loud, you'll find the power they have over you evaporates.

3. Reframe your mindset. Your goal isn't to avoid failure, it's to quickly recognize failure, what you could have done to succeed, and pivot quickly.

RESOURCES

- David Goggins, *Can't Hurt Me: Master Your Mind and Defy the Odds* (Austin: Lioncrest, 2018).
- Ryan Holiday, *The Obstacle Is the Way: The Timeless Art of Turning Trials into Triumph* (New York: Portfolio/Penguin, 2014).
- Mark Manson, *The Subtle Art of Not Giving a*

F*ck: A Counterintuitive Approach to Living a Good Life (New York: HarperCollins, 2016).

SUCCESS

Ten years after I started Intrinium, the business was generating a consistent profit. We had been making money for a while, but with the pillars in place and our culture in order, we really hit our stride. I was able to pay off debts and was living comfortably. With a good amount of discretionary income, I couldn't help but think, "What should I do with my money?"

I could have bought a bunch of expensive crap—trappings of a rich life. That just wasn't me, though. I was just trying to live a normal life, and still am. I want to take care of the people in my life, live well, and retire well someday. So I didn't splurge on anything fancy—didn't go on a shopping spree on Rodeo Drive. I just sat on it. Then one day, just before the holidays, an opportunity landed in my lap.

To get ready for our family's Christmas party every year, we do a kind of secret Santa, drawing a name for the person we'll give a gift to. Our variation is that instead of choosing the gift, we have to buy something from that person's wish list. One family member, Mandy, drew the name of my fiancée, Kylie, whose Amazon list included an inflatable dinosaur costume (yeah, it sounds weird, but she's a nerd, what can I say?).

Mandy is the single mother of an autistic child. She was waiting tables when she became a mother at age twenty. She doesn't have much income, so she had to choose a less expensive gift on the list. At the party, Mandy confided to Kylie, "I really wanted to get you that costume, but it was like seventy dollars and I just couldn't afford it."

I heard that and immediately thought, *She can't afford to spend seventy dollars. In my world, I likely wouldn't notice if seventy bucks disappeared from my account.* I found out that a lot of Mandy's pay goes toward a car payment, and it's not even an expensive one. Spokane doesn't have a functional public transit system, so you need a car to go anywhere. She lives with her parents and spends most of her time at home taking care of her child. Childcare, especially for a child with special needs, is expensive. Mandy wants to move herself and her child into a home of their own, but until she pays off the car loan, she can't save enough for the down payment.

After I found this out, I pulled her parents aside and asked them, "It sounds like Mandy's life would change if someone just paid off her car loan. Is that right?" They said, "It's not as though she would be rich, but she would be able to move out and move her life forward."

That year, I decided to break with tradition. I didn't pull Mandy's name for our secret Santa exchange, but I got her something anyway: I paid off the balance on her car loan.

Within six months, Mandy's life did change. She used the extra money she had every month to help her boyfriend fix up his place, which they then sold for a profit and got their own home that's big enough for all three of them. As I write this, wedding plans are in the works.

I also had the opportunity a few years later to help another family member, a massage therapist I'll call Cheryl, who came down with substantial health issues. Because she required frequent operations, Cheryl was often unable to work, and without work, she could not pay her monthly mortgage. She worried about having to leave the house and move back in with her parents. So I bought the mortgage from the bank and negotiated a deal where she pays me when she can. This relieved her from the worry of losing the place, and it hasn't hurt me financially.

Years later, every time I see Mandy, she thanks me. So does Cheryl. That wasn't my goal, but I have to admit, I get a lot of satisfaction from being in a position where I can help people I care about, who need help. In my mind, that's one of the best reasons to become financially successful. It's great to have a nice house, a nice car, and all that other stuff you think you'll want while you're working your way up. But when I think about how much cash I've dropped on random bullshit, I know that's not what I was working for. Helping family members has brought me more satisfaction than anything I could do with my money for myself.

HIDDEN REWARDS

It's hard to start and run a business. At times, you feel like yelling, *"Why the fuck am I even bothering?!"* For a long time, I didn't know why, but I finally figured it out. Success has huge rewards beyond the obvious ones and far beyond what you can imagine.

When I started Intrinium and thought about what success would look like, all I could picture were material things: a million dollars in the bank, a big house on a hill, and a four-car garage filled with Ferraris.

As I became able to afford some expensive things, I came to the realization that owning things doesn't always make you happy, and owning too many things can make you very unhappy. The stuff you buy owns *you*, not the other way around. That's not where your potential for real joy lies.

TAKE YOUR TIME

One thing that success brought me is a lifestyle that lets me set my own schedule. How many hours I work is separate from how much revenue the business earns. Because my company is stable and has great leadership from my executive and management teams, I can say, "I'm going to spend next week in the mountains doing whatever the heck I want to do. Outside of driving into town to make a few calls, I'm not going to work." I'm confident that when I come back to the office, I won't be walking into chaos.

Taking the time to enjoy the fruits of your labor, instead of constantly laboring in your business, frees your mind to discover what else success can do. It allows you to improve your quality of life in many ways, but only if you take the initiative to do so.

MEET PEOPLE WHO INTEREST YOU

Being a successful business owner gives you access to people you would never have met in any other position. I can pick up the phone and call the mayor, or the CEO of one of the biggest consulting firms in town and they take my call. I can ask them to lunch and they accept. When you run a company, people notice. They see you differently. Sometimes they see you for the first time. These connections can present other opportunities, such as investing in other businesses and participating in charity events. You start to see yourself differently, too. That, in turn, empowers you to do more in the world than you ever could as an employee.

HELP YOUR COMMUNITY, YOUR INDUSTRY, THE WORLD

Your newfound credibility empowers you to affect positive change. You can leverage your success for the good of yourself, your family, your colleagues and employees, your customers, your vendors, your community—and the world.

People who become successful have an obligation to show gratitude to the community and use their money for good. That includes helping out your family and friends in need, lifting up struggling businesses, donating to social or political causes, and giving your staff fair market wages and high-quality benefits.

Beyond mentoring, I don't do a lot of hands-on charitable work at this point. For now, most of my contributions have been financial, as prior to the COVID-19 pandemic, I was frequently traveling, either for work or for recreation. Someday I'll find the right cause to dedicate some time to, but for now, I'm happy to write checks for those causes I want to support.

Once you—and I—make the commitment to do more, and you've freed up the time, there are plenty of volunteer opportunities. Do whatever moves you the most. That's one of the benefits of being a business owner.

LIFT UP OTHER START-UPS

At a certain point in your career, you've gained skills and valuable experience that you can pass on to others just starting the journey. The credibility that came along with your success means they'll listen to you. I consider it my responsibility to help out with business incubators, and people who are working on their own start-ups. Because I'm earning enough in my business that I can afford to give this help on a pro bono basis.

In mastermind groups, I like to identify the members who are at the early stages of their business. Maybe they have ten people and a million dollars in revenue, but the revenue isn't consistent, and they aren't scaling. One thing I ask them, right out of the gate, is "What are you building?" I ask these young business leaders about their mission, vision, and values. I also work with them on their long-term growth plan, always asking "What do you want to get out of this business?" To coach and support them, I give them my cell phone number and invite them to contact me with questions or to just bounce an idea off me.

Seeing what a moderately successful veteran CEO's job looks like can help them understand whether that's a path they want to travel. Too many up-and-comers think they're going to be an overnight success, becoming billionaires à la Kylie Kardashian. It doesn't work like that in real life, and I tell them so.

Do they all decide they want to continue to pursue being a CEO? Absolutely not. Maybe half of the people I've mentored have concluded that starting or scaling a business isn't for them. I probably saved them a lot of pain because it didn't take them years to reach that decision. But the other half is still scaling, still in touch, and still grateful to the guy who helped them figure out "this culture thing."

LIFT UP YOUR STAFF

Use your experience and power to help your employees realize their goals. A lot of employers have the idea that their staff members should work for them forever, and they take it personally when people move on. I don't see things that way at all. When people leave your business and go on to do amazing things, that further defines your own success.

A few years after I started Intrinium, I hired a guy who went from being a part-time computer programmer who wasn't sure what he wanted to do with his life to becoming the chief security officer for one of the best-ranked healthcare systems in the nation. That evolution came about because in the eight years he worked with us, we taught him everything we knew about security, risk management, and leadership. By the time one of our clients needed a CSO, we placed him into that role as a contractor, and they ultimately hired him at a very substantial salary.

A few years back, I received a $12.5-million offer for Intrinium, a whole lot of money, no doubt. But I turned it down flat because I was certain the would-be buyer planned to move the contracts to another firm and lay off my staff. *That's* not what success looks like to me. It's not a way to screw the very people who worked so hard to get the business to this point. I'm only here because of them, and the money wouldn't make up for the fact that it came at a cost of putting fifty people out of work.

When you've gone through all the pain and failure it takes to get to a consistent level of success, you'll be faced with these kinds of ethical choices. When the time comes, what are you going to do? Are you going to take care of the people who took care of you? Or are you just going to cut and run? Something to think about.

GIVE BACK

If you've decided to start and grow your business, you've set out on a worthwhile journey. Once you reach your definition of success, you can be sure that you didn't get there by yourself. Your staff, your customers, your family, and your community contributed to where you are today. I hope you'll consider it your moral responsibility to look for opportunities to show your gratitude.

I'm not saying you have to give away all your wealth. But take really good care of the people in your life and your community. It's the right thing to do. When I started my business in 2007, I never realized that someday I would have the money and the power to do what I can now do. You'll never get as much joy out of counting the zeros on your bank statement as you will from helping people. It's a terrific feeling.

QUESTIONS, ACTIONS, AND RESOURCES

Success has a lot to offer the leader who sees beyond the obvious financial gains. Consider what you'll do with the time, money, and even the status earned as a business owner or leader. Don't squander these "riches"; invest them in people and causes you believe in and you'll find even greater fulfillment in your work and your life.

QUESTIONS

1. Success is a broad word. What is your definition, and what are your metrics for knowing you've achieved your definition?

2. What will you do with your success to help others? Use this moment to define a vision you can stick behind when the going gets tough.

3. Who is your Accountability partner that will ensure you won't get swept away into the grind of "more, more, more?"

ACTIONS

1. Take an action today to lift up someone else. Give back knowledge, time, money, or whatever you feel is appropriate to help another. Right now.

2. Write down what a day in your life looks like when you've achieved your definition of success. Be specific, take your time. Share it with your Accountability partner.

3. Find a mentor, an Accountability partner, or a coach.

RESOURCES

- The Arbinger Institute, *Leadership and Self-Deception: Getting out of the Box* (Oakland: Berrett-Koehler, 2018).
- Tom Bilyeu, *Impact Theory Podcasts* https://impacttheory.com
- Angela Duckworth, *Grit: The Power of Passion and Perseverance* (New York: Scribner, 2016).

CONCLUSION

How many times can one guy fuck up and still make it? I chalked up a *ton* of major mistakes when I was young and desperate—and also when I was more experienced and thought I was being smart. It took me years of bad decisions to learn enough to write about it in a book. I'm accountable for all of it. Every last screwup.

Now that you've heard my story, I hope you'll skip all the kicks in the ass my ignorance served up to me. If you were paying attention, you now know to hire the right people, prioritize culture, and heed any screaming red flags around a potential partner. Here's what else you now know that I didn't.

WHAT LEADERSHIP IS

Leadership is helping others meet their goals while also meeting yours. It's taking responsibility for the negative outcomes and recognizing your team for positive ones. Be aware of the challenges, acknowledge the failures, and keep promoting your vision. Never accept the status quo.

FIRST MANAGE YOURSELF

You can't lead people until you take the time and maybe the pain to figure out who you really are and what you really want. Part of managing yourself is doing whatever it takes to get control over parts of your personality that can get in the way. Everyone has stuff to overcome. It could be something like depression or laziness. For me, it's anxiety and mania, which I've controlled by a mix of strategies that promote self-awareness: meditation, working out, nutrition, time off, journaling, and therapy.

PARTNERSHIPS CAN BE A MINEFIELD

Run away fast, unless you're absolutely sure that person shares your goals for the business and your definition of success. And don't just take their word for it. Do your due diligence. Be as careful picking a business partner as you would a mate. If you don't leave your ego and emotions out of it, you could find yourself in a mess.

DON'T HIRE YOUR FRIENDS

Friends aren't going to do a great job or share your values just because they're your friends. All you're likely to get out of that extremely bad decision is a bunch of people who blur your judgment and expect favors. Sooner or later, you'll have to move them on and you might lose them as friends. It's not worth it. The workforce you need should be made up of qualified strangers you can set clear expectations with and hold accountable.

CULTURE ENABLES BUSINESS

Clearly outlined mission, vision, and values guide every decision you and your team have to make. They'll let the business run without your involvement in every day-to-day micro detail. They're also a touchstone to remind yourself, your staff, and your clients of who you are as a company. Because of the role of a healthy culture in aiming everyone in the same direction, it will reduce your stress level while it raises your success. I would never start another business without laying out the culture.

FAILURE IS A LEARNING OPPORTUNITY

Failure is an opportunity, if you can learn from it. Don't deny it or treat it as something to fear, but rather something to examine. Assault it head-on. That's the only way to keep from repeating the same mistakes. Failure's most valuable purpose is to show you how to improve. Stare it in the face, and ask, "How can we learn from what happened so we can do better next time?" Then act on your answers.

SUCCESS IS WHAT YOU MAKE IT

Your bank account shouldn't be the only thing that grows when you get your company where you want it. I hope you'll realize you have an obligation to give back. Put your position, experience, and resources to work on helping your family and community. You'll find it feels great to leverage what you created in your business to help create a better world.

ARE YOU UP FOR IT?

Still want to run a company? Be a CEO? Lead a group of people toward a mission and a vision, instilling proper values along the way?

If you're up for it, just remember it's all on you. The good, the bad, and the ugly. Take responsibility for everything that happens. When you stop owning it, you relinquish your power.

Personal Accountability defines me as a leader. I've made a lot of mistakes and learned a lot of lessons too. And I've discovered that Accountability, for a leader, is everything. It's the core message of this book, as I hope you've seen.

If you'd like to share your experiences as a leader, feel free to reach out. Let's have a conversation. I'm always open to hearing about the new challenges other CEOs are facing and ways they've discovered to deal with them. Connect with me at www.nolangarrett.co. I guarantee you Integrity, Respectful Candor, and above all, Accountability.

ACKNOWLEDGMENTS

Nothing triggers impostor syndrome more than publishing a book—your first book—that's pretty much just about your failures. Thank you to the entire Scribe team for the encouragement and support to make publishing this book possible. Susan in particular, thank you for all of your hard work helping my words reach the page in a consumable form.

Kylie, my fiancée, thank you for your patience while I worked through many edits, rewrites, tweaks, and "what about..." conversations. You're my favorite-est person and I love you. And Nick, who ultimately became my best friend while suffering all of these early-years mistakes with me—thank you for everything.

And to each of my staff, past and present—I wouldn't have had the opportunity to learn so much if it weren't for your support and understanding.

Jeff—my original business partner at Intrinium. Intrinium wouldn't exist without those late nights and the hard effort you put in to help get us off of the ground. Despite parting ways in the early years, my appreciation for your efforts has not faded with time.

To my executive team—Pat, Stephen, Bobbie, and Joshua, my gratefulness for your trust in my leadership is boundless. It's an honor to work with such a high-quality executive team.

Much of Intrinium's early years wouldn't have been successful if it weren't for Conrad. Thank you, Conrad, for all of your efforts with Intrinium during those times.

And to two mentors I've had the most incredible luck to meet—Steve and Marty. Both of you have helped shaped my leadership capabilities in ways that are difficult to express, and I cannot describe my appreciation for your mentorship and your friendship.

I also wish to thank Ted Schmidt, of ActionCOACH Spokane. Ted, you were invaluable in rebuilding the Intrinium culture around our pillars coaching me as I navigated the partnership challenges we were experiencing. Thank you, so much.

And finally, to Intrinium's clients, many of which have been such for more than a decade. Thank you for the risk you took on a twenty-three-year-old kid who seemed to know a couple of things about cybersecurity and risk management. The trust you placed in me ultimately launched my leadership and business journey, and I am forever grateful.

—NOLAN GARRETT, DECEMBER 2020

ABOUT THE AUTHOR

NOLAN GARRETT is the CEO of Intrinium, an information technology and cybersecurity consulting and management firm he founded in 2007. The company's awards include 2020 Inc. 5000 Fastest Growing Private Companies, 2019 ActionCOACH Best Growth, and 2019 and 2018 Best Place to Work in the Inland Northwest from the *Journal of Business*. Nolan himself is a highly experienced and certified cybersecurity and technology practitioner with a broad range of multi-industry experience.

Nolan's clients include some of the top-ranked healthcare, financial services, and retail organizations in the United States, spanning from coast to coast. Many of his clients require a non-disclosure agreement due to the sensitivity of the information security work performed, and therefore shall remain unnamed. In addition, he has acquired three businesses and merged them into Intrinium, expanding his business's capabilities each time.

Nolan has been published in such forums as the *Forbes Technology Council*, and he is often invited to speak at various industry and association conferences. In his spare time, he builds drones, plays guitar and video games, drives fast (and/or old) cars, picks up heavy things and puts them back down again, and experiments with home automation and the Internet of Things (IoT). He lives in Spokane, Washington, with his fiancée, Kylie.

CPSIA information can be obtained
at www.ICGtesting.com
Printed in the USA
FSHW012305131021
85452FS

9 781544 518817